finding my Irish

Katherine Murphy Cahill's (Aunt Kate) wedding band.

finding my Irish

Sharon Shea Bossard

Finding My Irish
Copyright © 2005 by Sharon Shea Bossard

International Standard Book Number: 0-9767579-0-7
Library of Congress Control Number: 2005928801

Disclaimer: Some of the names of the people have
been changed at their request, and any similarities to actual
persons, either living or dead, are merely coincidental.

PRINTED IN THE UNITED STATES OF AMERICA

Shea
Publications
P.O. Box 238
Lake Zurich, IL 60047
www.findingmyirish.com

To my beautiful daughter Jennifer, so that she may know them, embrace their memory, and love them for their sacrifices.

Table of Contents

My Parents

Epilogue

Acknowledgments

To my brothers Jim and John, I proudly present the book you suggested I write and to my sister Bonnie, without whose love and support I could never have continued; she convinced me I could, and to her son, my nephew, Dr. Marc Travis, for his expert consultation.

To my cousin Mary Stevens for sharing Hannah's letter, our grandmother's book, and family documents. To my cousin Eleanor Walsh and her husband Al for the valuable information about Omaha.

To John and Kitty Murphy, how can I ever thank you for all that you have given me? Not only did I find family, I also discovered the deep love and affection that families reserve only for each other. Sister Bertilla, you are a blessing. I'm so glad we're cousins.

To Patrick O'Leary, John Francis O'Sullivan and Kathleen Corless, Mary O'Neil from Valentia; Phyllis Beirne from Boyle and all the others who helped throughout this amazing adventure.

To all my friends who suffered through chapters while I struggled to make sense of them—thank you for your patience and time. Jeff Clery, thanks for convincing me that being Irish is special.

A heartfelt thank you to the Barrington Writer's Group for their valuable support and assistance; a very special thank you to Miriam Lykke, who guided and helped me through the rough spots and pushed me to learn more than I thought possible.

And last but not least, to my incredible husband, to whom I owe everything, for without him this book would not have been possible. Thank you, Phil, for always loving me and being proud.

Family Tree

Sharon Shea Bossard
1945

Father
Mike Carberry Shea
1900 – 1975

Mother
Helen J. Healy
1912 – 1988

Grandfather
Michael Shea
1859 – 1925

Grandmother
Bridget Murphy
1865 – 1913

Grandfather
Michael Healy
1879 – 1950

Grandmother
Sarah Burns
1881 – 1966

Great-
Grandmother
Julia Falvey
?

Great-
Grandmother
Mary Connor
1833 - 1912

Great-
Grandmother
Ellen Healy
1844 – 1896

Great-
Grandmother
Mary Higgins
1842 – 1896

Great-
Grandfather
Michael Shea
?

Great-
Grandfather
John Murphy
1823 - 1916

Great-
Grandfather
William Healy
1806 – 1910

Great-
Grandfather
John Beirne
1837 – 1897

Ireland

CHAPTER 1

The Journey

March 2003

My two brothers, my sister, and I are 100% Irish-American. Surnames such as Shea, Murphy, Healy, and Beirne perch themselves precariously on the branches of our family tree—all of this Irish and no family history to share with our children. Growing up in the western suburbs of Chicago in the early 1950s, we'd overhear conversations about the Irish counties of Roscommon and Kerry at the few family gatherings we attended, but those places were as foreign to us as the families we visited. We knew little of our family background except that our relatives had led terribly sad lives. What we did learn at a very young age from arguments, accusations, rumors, and whispers was that to be Irish meant to be defensive and secretive. We had to learn to be firm and brave. Heartbreak—it would seem—was a stone's throw away. My mother advised me never to marry an Irishman. "It's time to break the strain," she always said. I grew up believing that if I were foolish enough to marry into an Irish family, then I deserved all the misery that would come with it.

One might assume that growing up in an Irish-American household meant an observance of a St. Patrick's Day that would rival New Year's Eve—but not so in our family! Every year, my loyal mother honored Ireland's patron saint by fastening green satin ribbons to our school uniforms. When we arrived home, the aroma of cooked cabbage greeted us. And when the last limp, gray leaf was eaten and the pot scrubbed and stored, Helen Healy paid homage to all the saints of Ireland with an elaborate celebration of her own. She'd ceremoniously pour herself a good stiff Irish whiskey, sit at her well-polished baby grand piano, and play the Irish melodies handed down through her father. Twilight cast a ghostly shadow on the wall, creating the illusion of another poor soul sharing in her hopeless night of mournful memories. When she sang *Toora-Laural-Lura, That's an Irish Lullaby*, it made me crumble inside. That haunting tune possessed an all-consuming power that draped a curtain of lingering sadness around me.

My father, Mike Shea, never connected emotionally with any of us. He remained a distant figure by leaving early in the morning for work and returning late so that he could eat his supper in private. When I was eight, I remember resting my head on his lap while he read the newspaper. I can still recall his scratchy wool trousers biting into my cheek; I willingly endured the irritation just to be close to him.

We never knew my father's parents, nor did we know until recently that he had four older brothers and two sisters and that they had grown up in Omaha, Nebraska. His mother, Bridget, died in 1913 when he was thirteen years old. His father, Michael, died in 1925, the body discovered in the Missouri River one foggy April morning.

My mother's parents lived in Chicago. With each visit, our mother cautioned us not to get too comfortable because we never knew when the scene might turn ugly and hasten our departure. Her mother, Sarah Healy, died in 1966; her father, Michael Healy, in 1950. My mother adored her father, and his death, I believe, was her undoing.

Recently, while feeling brave and thinking myself absurdly foolish for fearing the Irish melodies of my youth, my husband and I purchased a CD of Irish music in preparation for our first family trip to Ireland. The minute the tenors began to sing the haunting melodies, my fingers clenched the car seat and my tears flowed. I was carried back to the year 1950; I was five years old again. Turning my face towards the window, I felt foolish and embarrassed for crying. What I knew to be a painful childhood memory resurfaced and with the same traumatic intensity— nothing had changed! It was then I realized the unexpressed sadness within me when it came to anything Irish.

I began my search for my grandparents, Michael and Sarah Healy, by scrolling through the Ellis Island website and locating the name of the ship on which my mother's parents arrived in 1903. I later learned from searching records at the Family History Center in Salt Lake City that my father's parents entered through Castle Gardens, New York in 1880. I mailed letters to all of the Shea families in Omaha, Nebraska, asking if they recognized the name of my father. I received one response. It was from my father's brother's daughter—my first cousin, Eleanor.

Next, I followed up on an address my brother had given me for a Mary Stevens in Washington. Having no idea about her relationship to us, I wrote to ask if she knew my Shea family. Her response arrived within the week. Her mother was a Shea and Mary was my first cousin. Both of these wonderful newfound cousins provided important bits of information. I learned that my father's parents were born in Valentia and Cahersiveen, County Kerry, Ireland.

My husband, Phil, our daughter, Jennifer, and I looked forward to a well-deserved vacation. We planned to show Jennifer the Irish countryside of her great-grandparents. If we found the counties and towns of my grandparents' births, we might stop to take a few pictures, but I hadn't yet gathered enough information to do a thorough search for my family history in Ireland. So I accepted the fact that, rather than a mission to explore, this trip would be a pleasure jaunt. The task of searching for traces of my grandparents could wait for another trip—or so we thought. We had no idea how Ireland would capture us and change our lives forever.

We were scheduled on the seven o'clock flight from Chicago to Shannon with a stop in Dublin. We packed light in order to avoid checking any luggage. I studied the tourist map to make sure we wouldn't miss anything of interest on our six-day holiday.

We couldn't sleep because the lively chatter from restless passengers kept us awake for most of the night. I looked out the window and caught a faint glimmer of sunrise. We seemed to be floating on a sea of clouds waiting to be bathed in the sunlight of a new day. The plane bounced and creaked, the seat belt indicator chimed, and passengers hurried to their seats in preparation for landing.

We stopped at the gate; the engines were silenced. Echoing through the cabin were the irritating sounds of luggage being dragged from overhead and the cries of cranky children being herded toward the exit door. We stayed put until a different crew boarded to take us on the Shannon. Grateful for the peace and quiet, we settled in for a relaxing ride to the West Coast of Ireland.

Huge gray clouds swallowed up the sun's rays. I recalled packing our umbrellas and tried to remember where they were for quick retrieval, once we landed. Just then the weather changed, and the sun filtered through the windows. The sunshine and clear skies gave us incredible aerial views of Ireland. Emerald-colored pastures were sprinkled with variegated hues of green grass dripping golden colored dew. Ireland was dressed in all of its grandeur to greet its visitors.

On our descent, I noticed small white circles dotting the landscape. Dozens of white fluffy sheep grazed lazily in the sun-streaked fields. Herds of sheep, cattle, and horses came into view; we glided effortlessly over them. Small farmhouses with smoke circling their chimneys were scattered throughout the countryside, and billowing white clouds settled into their morning routine. The serene beauty of Ireland captivated and fascinated me. The faint sound of chimes signaled us to fasten our seat belts for our arrival into Shannon.

From the airport, we drove south to Limerick and east towards Waterford. True to our itinerary, we visited the woolen mills, the crystal factory, centuries-old cathedrals, and even kissed the Blarney Stone. We enjoyed staying in the B & B's that were scattered throughout the countryside and even got to spend a couple of nights in a farmhouse. The Irish breakfast of cereal, eggs, sausage, bacon, toast, fruit, and tea were filling and most welcome. Each day brought a new adventure, and we were thoroughly enjoying our visit.

On the morning of our fifth day, we happened upon the seaport of Cobh in County Cork. Our plan was to avoid some of the larger, busier cities and stick to the coastal areas. Road signs directed us to the Emigrant Museum, and we decided to stop for a tour. While Phil parked the car, I noticed a sign above the door of the museum that read "The Queenstown Story." I had just recently learned that Queenstown was the port of departure for all four of my grandparents and couldn't believe my good fortune in having found it.

We joined a virtual reality tour that retraced the steps of the 2.5 million adults and children who emigrated from Ireland on the coffin ships, the early steamers, and the great ocean liners. We "witnessed" the deplorable conditions on board those ships and vicariously experienced their perilous journey. The thunder of the raging, treacherous sea mixed with the voices of the terrified emigrants echoed throughout the large exhibit hall. Overcome by emotion, I escaped through a side door, for I had seen and heard enough. Once outside, my thoughts were interrupted by the piercing, pitiful cries of the seabirds and by the rolling waves that slammed into the dock, causing it to creak and shudder.

Gazing across the channel to where huge ships once waited for the arrival of the tenders filled with the emigrants, I thought about the poor Irish families—my family—who had gathered on the same pier where I now stood.

I heard my daughter's footsteps, and I knew that Phil was close behind. When I turned towards them, they could see by the look on my face that things had changed. Our visit to the Emigrant Museum helped to re-define our trip. We were no longer tourists, but seekers of family history. Phil and Jennifer expressed their support in helping me find my Irish. With only one day of vacation left, we headed for Cahersiveen, County Kerry, for now, we truly had a mission.

The rugged scenery was breathtaking. Giant waves crashed into the unguarded coastline. Lush, green fields, splashed with daffodils, leaned into the gentle breezes that filtered through the valley. Driving along the coast, we marveled at how well each village had maintained its old world charm.

When we entered the quaint little seaside village of Cahersiveen, we noticed an inviting old pub. Spirited colors of green and yellow gave the place a welcoming look, and a sign above the door read, "O'Driscoll's." The pleasurable aroma of good food drifted into our car, causing our stomachs to rumble. In our haste to get to Cahersiveen, we had forgotten to eat, so Phil parked the car and we hurried inside. Locating a table close to the peat fire, we checked out the bar menu: bacon and cabbage, fish and chips, meat pie, Irish stew, and cheeseburgers with chips. We ordered the cheeseburgers and settled in to enjoy a hearty lunch.

The barkeeper inquired about our vacation and asked if we were enjoying ourselves. I told him that my grandfather was born in Cahersiveen in 1859 and that he had left for America in 1880. And with that the barkeeper said something I'll never forget, "Welcome Home!" I asked if he knew anything about the Shea family I was seeking. He laughed and said he was sure he did, all two hundred of them. He then went on to tell us that the name O'Shea was a very old name in Cahersiveen, and we would be sure to find many Sheas on the drive through town.

We gathered our coats and left to search for any trace of my grandparents. Once out on the street, we were surprised to see how many shops displayed the name O'Shea above their doors. This was, indeed, the town of my grandfather.

We passed small grocery stores bustling with customers, numerous pubs, dry cleaners, and several florist shops. An Internet cafe caught Jennifer's attention, so we went inside. Phil took that opportunity to walk to the Heritage Center in search of any family information.

Seated inside the cozy cafe, I felt suddenly overwhelmed by the task at hand. I had no idea where to begin. Then I noticed a huge old stone church across the street from the cafe. Thinking that it might have been the parish of my grandparents, I mumbled something to Jennifer and rushed out the door.

After climbing dozens of steps, I finally reached the grand entrance. The heavy wooden door slammed shut behind me, causing the few old women scattered around the church to turn in obvious displeasure. I waited for them to resume their prayers before moving forward. The church was magnificent. Beautifully polished marble floors reflected the sun's rays pouring through the stained-glass windows, creating a kaleidoscope of color that danced on the tiles. Dark walnut confessionals stood like fortresses in the impressive vestibule. Walking up the side aisle, I glanced over at the pious old women whose rosary beads dangled from their thick fingers, their pale, aged hands stark against their long-sleeved black woolen dresses. I heard their whispered prayers. Feeling chilled, I wrapped my coat tightly around myself and marveled at the devotion of these parishioners to tolerate such an icebox.

Rounding a corner, I approached a door that was slightly ajar with a sign overhead identifying it as the Clerk's Office. I knocked softly. Tim Casey introduced himself and ushered me inside his small office. He stood just over five feet with snow-white hair and bright blue eyes; he appeared to be in his eighties. His relaxed yet official manner suggested that he often received visitors from America who were looking for their ancestors.

Tim informed me that the Daniel O'Connell Church was built in 1888 and had the distinction of being one of three Catholic Churches in the world named after a layperson. The name of the church slipped past me, as I was discouraged by the date. Surely this couldn't be the church of my grandparents because Michael was born in 1859 and Bridget in 1865.

Then Phil and Jennifer appeared as if out of nowhere. I hadn't expected them; they told me that the clerk's voice and my voice carried to the back of the church, making it easy to find me. I felt sorry for the old women who were trying to say their prayers, but maybe they were used to being interrupted by Americans who visited their church in the relentless search for ancestors. Finding any trace of my grandparents might not be possible; too many years had passed.

We enjoyed listening to the melodic rhythms of Tim's brogue and his wonderful stories of Cahersiveen. Nothing much had changed since his boyhood days. The people had grown older and some of the children were long gone for other parts of the world in search of their fortunes. Tour buses rumbled through the town, and computers had found their way into the schools and the public library. Other than that, life was blissfully serene in this centuries-old town. The beauty of the rugged coastline with the surf dancing its way to the rocky shore continued every day, just as it had since the beginning of time.

Tim explained that the Daniel O'Connell Church had replaced the old church that was probably the parish of my grandparents. He then ushered us into another room where volumes of old church records were stored. Choosing a large ledger-type book, Tim carefully placed it on the table in front of us; faded gold lettering identified it as 1850 Church Records. The ancient leather book with its pages yellowed and torn looked as though it belonged in a temperature-controlled museum. Tim invited us to look through it, but I was hesitant to even breathe on it for fear it would disintegrate.

Carefully we turned each crumbling page in search of the baptism records for Michael Shea and Bridget Murphy, noticing that many of the pages were either missing or badly faded. I went through the book one more time just in case I overlooked something. Tim told us about how he had helped many people from America find their Irish ancestors, but he didn't think this was going to happen quickly for me.

Not wanting to take leave of this kind gentleman too soon, I asked if he would have dinner with us at one of the pubs in town. A big smile spread across his face. I was sure he would accept our offer and was surprised when he said that he preferred to have his potato at home.

Disappointed, but otherwise cheered by meeting Tim, we left the church and drove out of town in search of a bed and breakfast. Off the Carhan Road, we discovered an ancient graveyard and decided to stop and read the names on the old slabs. A misty ground fog weaved its way around each of the tombstones, giving the place a haunted look. We were relieved to see that others were visiting as well, for at least we wouldn't be alone while exploring the ancient, untended graveyard.

A plaque at the entrance to the Sugrena Famine Cemetery stated in detail the history of the graveyard. Buried there are the Irish who perished during the 1847 potato famine. There had been no proper burials. The bodies were either covered with dirt where they lay or dragged to nearby ditches and covered with brambles and stones. This explained the cascading dirt hills that lined the walls of the cemetery directly adjacent to the road. Many of the neglected tombstones were inscribed with the name Shea, which signified that Sugrena was part of my ancestral history. Focusing on the rocky terrain, we walked in silence; each of us chose a different path.

While wandering among the forgotten graves, I was approached by a tall, white-haired gentleman who offered to accompany me. He told me he lived in Dublin and that every year at this time he and his family made the pilgrimage to Sugrena. As we walked, he shared the history that led to the devastation and the deaths of the residents of Cahersiveen during the Great Famine of 1847. He explained that the bodies of the dead were too filthy or diseased, their stench too disgusting, and their faces too ravaged by rats and dogs for strangers to treat them with respect. When an entire family died in their thatched hut and the decomposing bodies were discovered, the cabin was simply knocked down over them and set on fire. That was the burial. Only when a dead person had a living relative dedicated and strong enough to carry, drag, or cart the body to the graveyard were they buried in the consecrated ground that all Irish Catholics hoped would be their final resting place.

He recalled stories of helpless people being too weak to care where their relatives were buried, as the living had already lost their ability to experience regret, to think of past pleasures, to long for relief from their distress, or to try to bury their loved ones. In the thatched huts where stench from death and disease burned like phosphorus in their nostrils, the Irish experienced a hell determined not by God but by the British government. No one accused the English of causing the potato to rot, but the English government was guilty of the criminal neglect of millions of starving people.

He continued, telling me that people had eaten dogs, cats, and horses, and chewed on grasses torn from the barren fields. The truly desperate fed on human corpses. He then pointed to an old ruin in the pasture next to the graveyard—the Bahaghs Workhouse—the poorhouse where thousands of Irish were housed before, during, and after the famine. When the Irish could no longer pay the rent to the English landlord and the potato crop could no longer feed the family, they had no choice but to enter the workhouse. If they were too weak to make it to Bahaghs, they died of hunger on the side of the road. The famine of 1847 claimed 2.2 million lives.

Then he asked about my family and why I chose to visit Sugrena, as it wasn't a tourist spot. I was unable to say much, only that my father's parents were born in County Kerry and my mother's parents in County Roscommon. He asked me if I'd ever heard of a man named Daniel O'Connell, The Great Liberator, who was born in Cahersiveen in the late 1700s. He stated proudly that his name was also Daniel O'Connell, and the hero that he spoke of was his distant cousin, who was responsible for Ireland's first experiment in democracy. Frustrated with my inability to recall the name and realizing that I had no knowledge of history, he suggested that I study my history because I had a responsibility to be informed about Ireland's past. Before turning away, he told me to visit the church in Cahersiveen named after his cousin. Then I remembered where I heard the name. The church where I met Tim Casey was named for Daniel O'Connell.

Phil and Jennifer were waiting in the car for me, and they could see I was troubled. I told them about the incredible coincidence of meeting the distant cousin of Daniel O'Connell. They didn't, of course, recognize the name but went on to tell me about their conversations with his family. Jennifer learned the origin of the Irish heritage ring, depicting scenes from ancient Ireland, while

Phil acquired interesting details concerning the old graves. They enjoyed their time at Sugrena, but I was embarrassed by my lack of knowledge of Ireland's past. How could I begin to understand the struggles of my grandparents and their parents unless I knew Ireland's history?

We continued our drive through town and noticed the Cahersiveen Heritage Museum where Phil had gone earlier. After hearing my complaint that I did not know enough history of Ireland, he suggested a trip through the archives might prove valuable.

The building dated from 1870; artifacts and pictures of both past and present lined the walls. I looked carefully for the name of Michael Shea or Bridget Murphy. There was nothing! Facts regarding the famine era matched the stories that Mr. O'Connell told me in Sugrena, and I was overwhelmed by the sudden realization that my great-grandparents had survived the famine.

After leaving the museum, Phil and I knew we had much work ahead of us, for our visit to Cahersiveen strengthened our determination to find out about my grandparents' lives in Ireland.

Our journey was coming to an end. We didn't have time to visit County Roscommon; that would have to wait for another trip. We talked through most of the night about how we needed to locate documents from Ireland as well as from America in order to find any traces of their lives.

My fear of letting anything Irish into my life had kept me away from this beautiful place far too long, and it was now time for me to embrace my heritage.

CHAPTER 2

In Dublin, Fair City

November 2003

Eight months had passed since our visit to Ireland, and we were preparing for our return trip. I recalled how difficult the task of tracing family seemed then. But this time, with copies of all the documents necessary to begin our search, we were well prepared.

We had made several visits to the National Archives and Records Administration in Chicago and located the Ship Manifest from Ellis Island for my mother's parents. Vital records from the State of Connecticut gave us information on my grandparents' marriage and the births of three of their children. We traveled to the Family History Center in Salt Lake City, Utah, where we searched microfilm from Ireland for information on birth, baptism, marriage, the 1901 Irish Census, as well as the ship records for Bridget Murphy and Michael Shea. We traveled to Omaha, Nebraska, researching documents pertaining to the Shea family. Articles retrieved from old newspapers in the Omaha library gave us the details surrounding their deaths.

I had mailed requests to Dublin for the birth certificates of my four grandparents, but I received only two—Michael Healy and Sarah Beirne. My family never knew that Sarah's last name had been changed from Beirne to Burns when she was processed through Ellis Island. It took months to figure that one out and only through the 1901 Irish Census were we able to locate the correct birth record. The birth certificates for Michael Shea and Bridget Murphy couldn't be located, so searching in Dublin for those birth or baptism records would be a priority. The United States Census records for the years 1900, 1910, and 1920 told us the year they entered America, their occupations, names, address, and the ages of all family members living in the household at the time of the census.

Approval from the Bishop in Killarney is required to search church records for County Kerry. With that approval letter safely tucked inside my briefcase, we were confident of our success in Ireland.

Phil and I arrived in Dublin on the early morning flight from Chicago. Rested and in good spirits, we picked up our rental car and proceeded into the city in search of our hotel. Joining early morning commuters into Dublin proved to be challenging but with patience and perseverance, we located our hotel. The Quality Inn was only a fifteen-minute bus ride to the City Center, so we parked the car in the underground garage because we wouldn't need it for the remainder of our stay in Dublin.

We checked into the hotel, stored our luggage in the room, and hurried out the door in order to arrive at the National Library when it opened. A light drizzle greeted us as we ran for the bus. Then the skies opened and rain poured down in bucketfuls, and I wondered if our small umbrella would be cover enough. From the shelter of our bus, we observed the heavy rain and blustery winds that whipped the pedestrians unmercifully. It appeared that staying on the bus for a city tour was wiser than venturing out, but we had much work to do in the few days we planned to stay in Dublin. From the National Library, we intended to visit the General Record Office, the Land Valuation's Office, and the National Archives. The rain would slow us down but not deter us from our itinerary.

The observant bus driver, hearing our concern, pulled close to the curb and wished us a good day. Departing the warmth of the bus, we juggled our leaking umbrella, and while checking the map for directions to the library, I tucked my briefcase under my jacket in an attempt to keep it dry. The incessant rain pelted us from all directions, our umbrella flew inside out, and we were thoroughly drenched. Water dripped into our shoes, our backs were wet, and the ink on our map was smudged. Pushed by the early morning crowd, we could see the library up ahead.

We sprinted towards the entrance. While shaking out my umbrella, I read the large plaque on the wall above the entryway. Founded in 1877, the library serves as the depository for over five million pieces of information covering genealogy, land trusts, and wills. A guard directed us to the coatroom, where we happily shed our rain-soaked jackets and stored our dripping umbrella. I proceeded to the Genealogy Department while Phil hurried off to look for old newspaper articles. We had recently learned that my great-grandfather, William Healy from County Roscommon, died in

1910 at the age of 104. Surely his death warranted an article in the Roscommon newspaper.

Seated comfortably in the Genealogy Section, I removed the Michael/Bridget file from my crowded briefcase. Enthusiastic groups of chatty people were clustered at various tables throughout the bright over-sized room. I overheard their conversations. They were Americans and, like us, hoped to find valuable information about their Irish ancestors. I knew they would leave hopelessly disappointed because they didn't have enough information for the researcher; all they had were last names. Without knowing the Irish county and townland of birth, it's just not possible to begin a search.

Our early arrival gave me the advantage of being first in line. The genealogist located the necessary microfilm information and then directed me to the second floor Reading Room. From my experience at the Salt Lake City Family History Center, I knew this would be a long and arduous task. Much of the vital information on the microfilm had either faded or been partially destroyed from the years of neglect, prior to their preservation.

I climbed the winding staircase to the Reading Room but became distracted by the complexity of the beautifully adorned stairwell, so I slowed my pace while turning to take it all in. The plaster walls were lavished in gold leaf pattern, and the high ceiling was decorated with figures of rosy-cheeked cherubs; their angelic presence provided me with the encouragement I needed to confront the monotony of the microfilms.

The Reading Room was magnificent, with a domed, frescoed ceiling, polished tables that stretched the width of the great room, and a collection of priceless leather-bound books. Soft lights added a warm glow to the comfortable surroundings; their illumination was reflected on the rich mahogany of the writing desks.

I noticed Phil at the Circulation Desk and quickly joined him. He was pleased to announce his find— William Healy's obituary. It revealed that my great-grandfather, who was born in 1806, had fought against the "English yoke" that subjugated the poor Irish farmer. He didn't live to see the treaty signed on December 6, 1921, to establish the Irish Free State, but he had survived long enough to acquire title to the three-room thatched cottage and the coveted land of his ancestors. Over one hundred people witnessed his burial in the centuries-old graveyard of Killarght in the town of Boyle, County Roscommon. Finding this incredible piece of family information provided the motivation for us to get started on the microfilms.

Phil and I collected ten small boxes of microfilm, located two reading machines, and sat down to scan miles of film in search of the baptismal record of Michael Shea. As we suspected, many of the films were either damaged or just unreadable because they were recorded in Latin. The civil birth records dating from before 1865 had been destroyed in the 1922 Civil War, so we had no choice but to rely on the baptismal records only. We concluded that Michael's baptismal certificate could very well be part of the destroyed records that were only partially copied.

After four hours, we decided to take a break from the tedium of the microfilm. We checked our agenda and decided to walk to the General Record Office to search for civil birth records. We hurried down the stairs to retrieve our coats and umbrella. Crowds jammed the cloakroom while long lines of patrons filled the vast assembly hall. We were delighted to see that the earlier downpour had become a gentle drizzle.

The streets of Dublin tend to confuse the visitor because the names change at every corner. Kildare Street turns into Lincoln Place, then it becomes Westland Row, and finally Lombard Street. We walked what we thought was a straight line but wasn't. Backtracking confirmed our suspicions, and we learned that we had to be very careful to follow our city map; we could easily get lost in Dublin and didn't have the time to spend going in circles.

The General Record Office was old and run-down. Our time spent in the National Library spoiled us because now we expected all government buildings to be palatial. In fact, we double-checked to make sure we were at the right place. Seeing our confusion and overhearing our concern, the security guard assured us we were, indeed, at the General Record Office and that all birth records were on the first floor. He asked us to take the steps because the elevator wasn't working. I inquired as to why the first floor would be located upstairs and he told us that we were at floor zero. Clearly confused, Phil and I made our way up the linoleum-clad stairs, being careful not to trip on the small chunks of plaster that had fallen from the base of the crumbling wall.

The place hummed with activity. Every seat was taken, and huge volumes were stacked on most of the tables. The fact that we could see no microfilm machines brought exaggerated sighs of relief from both of us. We found the books listing the years required for our search and began our hunt for the birth record of Bridget Murphy.

Two birth certificates emerged. One for a Bridget Murphy born on Valentia Island on January 15, 1865, and another for a Bridget Murphy born in Ballinskelligs, Cahersiveen on January 15, 1865. We ordered both to see if we could choose the correct one by checking Bridget's mother's maiden name. One cousin told me that Bridget's mother's maiden name was Sullivan, while another told me that Valentia Island was Bridget's birthplace. If we could find the birth record for a Bridget Murphy from Valentia with the mother's maiden name of Sullivan, that would be my grandmother.

We paid the fee of three Euros and waited for the two certificates. The minute the clerk called my name, I rushed to his desk to retrieve the documents. Phil and I immediately examined both of them:

> *Bridget Murphy, Valentia Island, Mother's Maiden Name: Connor*

and

> *Bridget Murphy, Ballinskelligs, Mother's Maiden Name: Sullivan*

This revelation presented us with a dilemma, since we were sure Bridget's birthplace was Valentia, but the Valentia Bridget didn't match the mother's maiden name of Sullivan. The only way we were going to solve this was to drive to County Kerry and visit each of the townlands. We weren't looking forward to the five-hour drive across Ireland, but we had no choice.

We checked our agenda to make sure all the work required in Dublin could be completed in a shortened period of time. We had scheduled a meeting with the genealogist from the National Archives, as well as a visit to the Valuation's Office for records on land ownership. How could we squeeze in a trip to County Kerry? We had one hour before the Valuation's Office closed for the day. Deciding to chance it, we ran to get there before closing time.

Snow and sleet poured down on us as we made our way across Dublin. We were surprised at how quickly we found the Valuation's Office, and were delighted to learn that we could conduct an independent search. We located the necessary documents, and Phil copied every page. I sorted papers, jotted notes, stapled, and placed the land deeds into my briefcase. Just as we finished our work, the Valuation's Office announced its closing. We gathered our belongings and headed out the door. The rain had stopped and the air was crisp, providing a welcome relief from the earlier nasty weather. Hungry, we headed to the local pub for some well-deserved food and relaxation.

Seated at the Temple Bar, we wolfed down a couple of orders of fish and chips generously doused with vinegar. We assessed the tasks we needed to complete before leaving Dublin for Ballinskelligs and Valentia. We listed our required stops, which included an independent tour of this beautiful city. I had heard so much about the Great Liberator Daniel O'Connell that I felt an obligation to visit the statue dedicated in his honor. Remembering my meeting with his distant cousin at the cemetery in Cahersiveen, I wished I had his address in Dublin; Mr. O'Connell would be pleased to know that I studied my Irish history.

We woke early the next morning so we could visit the National Archives and tour the Post Office. It was important to see the Post Office. An Irish person couldn't possibly think of visiting Dublin without entering the building where one of the bloodiest battles was waged against the British—the battle that would ultimately guarantee the rights of the Irish to govern their own state—the 1916 Easter Rising. We also found it necessary to return to the National Library to verify some of the information I had brought from home.

The General Post Office in Dublin houses an incredible array of art portraying the Easter Rising. Built in 1818, the GPO became a symbol of this famous battle. Members of the Irish Volunteers and Irish Citizen Army seized the building on Easter Monday, April 24, and Patrick Pearse read out the Proclamation of the Irish Republic from its steps. The rebels remained inside for almost a week, but shelling from the British eventually forced them out. Ireland must be the only country in the world where the most important historical building is its Post Office.

It continued to rain. The menacing Dublin sky was draped with thick, dense clouds, and we were ready to leave the crowded city for the clean, crisp air of the country. We headed for our hotel in order to get a good night's sleep before departing for Cahersiveen early the next morning. Remembering our visit last year with our daughter, we looked forward to returning to the quaint little town nestled alongside the Atlantic Coast.

Tomorrow couldn't arrive soon enough!

CHAPTER 3

Cahersiveen
Discovery

We departed Dublin a bit later than we had anticipated. After a breakfast delay, we quickly discovered that Friday morning traffic in Dublin matched a Chicago morning rush hour: crowds of commuters boarding buses, delivery trucks blocking traffic, and careless drivers weaving their way through the streets.

Once out of the city, the ride went smoothly. Phil expertly maneuvered our over-sized Ford on the narrow roads. Blue skies and bright sunshine encouraged and delighted us; we were almost convinced it rained every day in Ireland. Cheered by the good weather, we agreed the five-hour drive would go quickly.

It felt good to finally be in the country. We enjoyed seeing the plump sheep that grazed leisurely on hillsides; the early morning mist evaporated with the presence of the sun, and noticing the patchwork of wooded areas, increased our awareness of this beautiful island. We rolled through small villages early enough to observe groups of children walking to school, all of them neatly dressed in crisp uniforms. Church bells rang to announce the morning Mass. Bread-truck drivers blocked traffic to make their deliveries. It surprised us to see unwrapped loaves tossed onto the floor of the truck, only to be scooped up and taken into the stores.

Elderly men rode wobbly bicycles. Women pushed baby carriages along the narrow sidewalks, disappearing into the many shops along the way. Lorries crowded the too-narrow roads, and Phil had to pay close attention to make sure he stayed in the correct lane; there were a few instances when we almost drifted to the other side while making a left turn.

My legs were cramped and we both agreed that it was time to stop for gas and snacks. We couldn't find any pretzels, but there were plenty of vinegar potato chips. Small delis inside the gas stations made it convenient to grab a quick meal. We were making good time on our journey to Cahersiveen and planned to be there before noon. That would give us one entire afternoon and evening to find Bridget's birthplace and maybe also to locate my grandfather's townland.

With relief we finally entered County Kerry, watching closely for a sign indicating the road to Cahersiveen. Driving through the towns of Killarney, Killorglin, and Glenbeigh, we cheered, as we knew our destination was only minutes away. We were on a mission and the clock was ticking.

In Cahersiveen, we found a parking place in front of the local library and hoped the librarian could help us with our townland maps. Luckily, the library was empty of patrons, and the staff eagerly offered their assistance. The librarian spread our Ordinance Maps on the table and gave a brief synopsis of the area as well as explanations of words we didn't know. First, we asked what townlands were. She told us that townlands are unique to Ireland, and they are the smallest units of land used for administration. This word originally meant a rural residence protected by a palisade of stakes, a ditch, a thorn hedge, or a combination of all three. All areas of residence in the countryside are divided into townlands.

We were surprised to learn that we passed through the townland of Carhan Lower on our ride into the village. Carhan Lower was the birthplace of my grandfather. We then asked about the townlands of Allaghee More in Ballinskelligs and Ballyhearney in Valentia. She couldn't locate the townland of Allaghee More but was able to find Ballyhearney. She drew a yellow circle on our Ordinance Map and showed us the best way to get there. As for locating the townland of Allaghee More, she suggested we visit the Surveyor's Office in town.

The enormity of our task suddenly hit me, leaving me to wonder how we would ever accomplish all we had set out to do in less than one day. We were scheduled to leave Ireland tomorrow, and rushing around with so little time seemed counter-productive to our search, but then I considered that any little thread of information we found today would tie itself to something we'd already found. A weariness settled in, and thinking a little caffeine might help, I suggested we take a lunch break.

Phil noticed a small cafe tucked between two old buildings. It was crowded, but we managed to find seats by the window. We ordered sandwiches, and then sat back to watch the Friday afternoon shoppers. Ladies hurried along, carrying small bags of fresh vegetables. Tops of onions, carrots, and tomatoes nearly tumbled out of the bags. Small children ran alongside, barely keeping up with their mothers.

We watched out the window and ate. Phil looked over at me and commented that some of the women who passed the window resembled me. Amused by the comparison, I appreciated his words because these women looked healthy, with a rosy glow to their complexions and their soft shiny hair tousled by the wind. I imagined my grandparents walking past this very store over one hundred years ago, and I wondered about them and what their lives were like. Surely the store wouldn't have been a cafe back then, but it was a place they frequented; it was located in the middle of town. Checking the time, we emptied our trays and headed off to the Surveyor's Office.

The rickety, old building smelled of mildew and appeared to be vacant; the only sounds were our footsteps echoing off the wooden floors. The sound of papers rustling alerted us to an office up ahead, so we walked in that direction. We entered a small cubicle bursting with surveys and notebooks; loose papers were everywhere. An older man sat behind a spindle-legged desk. His glasses were balanced on the edge of his nose, and his thick hair was mussed. He got up quickly to greet us and listened carefully while we explained our dilemma regarding our two Bridgets. This seemed to be our lucky day. He knew of a local historian who had knowledge of the Ballinskelligs area, and he drew a map directing us to the cottage of Patrick O'Leary, a retired schoolteacher. He told us that

Patrick had studied the area of Ballinskelligs extensively and was familiar with every family, past and present.

We thanked him for his help and left to find Patrick. Outside it was raining hailstones and sleet—a wicked afternoon for a drive to Ballinskelligs.

Before heading for the coast, we decided to secure a bed and breakfast just in case we found ourselves out very late. This would also provide us with the opportunity to see the townland of Carhan Lower—the townland of my grandfather.

We located a charming B&B on a hilltop. Just as we arrived at the front door, the rain stopped, and the sun came out from behind the clouds. The view was breathtaking! There were mountains to the right, the Atlantic Ocean straight ahead, and green meadows at our feet. Double rainbows striped the deep blue sky; their colors were magnificent.

We secured a small room for the night. During a conversation with our host, I mentioned that my grandfather was born in Carhan Lower. She stepped back in surprise and pointed across the road. No cottage stood there now, only a lovely green pasture peacefully sharing space with tall grasses and wildflowers. She explained that my grandfather's townland was located by the groves of Carhan River nestled alongside the slopes of Beenatee and the Cnoc na dTobar Mountain. How wonderful to have found the place where my grandfather was born.

Phil and I walked across the road and into the field. I closed my eyes, trying to imagine the sound of my grandfather's voice and to feel his spirit. I was standing in the place where his cottage once stood, and I spoke to him as if he were there beside me.

"Michael, my grandfather, I have found you. This was where your journey began. Your youth was spent toiling in the fields while you felt hunger and despair. You dared to dream of a better life. Desperate, you walked for days to Queenstown to board the sailing vessel bound for America. How brave and strong you were to endure the emptiness in that one part of your heart you left in Ireland. Now, I speak to you and you answer, not in words that can be heard but those that can be felt. Dear Grandfather, though I never knew you, I am you!"

The breeze invited a birds' orchestra; the winds carried their sweet song. Clouds drifted over the abandoned wasteland that had watched the lowlands develop and change. It had seen a village grow where there was once vast woodland—it stands unchanged by time. The ground on which I stood had nourished my family for hundreds of years. It was the potato that grew in these fields; the potato that fed the pig to pay the rent, since paying the landlord came before the well being of the family.

The rain returned. Phil offered me space under the umbrella, and I accepted the comfort of the temporary shelter. We followed a path up the hill leading to a small church. Jagged rocks spilled into the neglected pasture.

Because my grandparents had lived by the sea, I assumed that my grandfather and his father were fishermen. But this wasn't the case. Treacherous currents, cliffs, rocks, and sudden squalls made it difficult to make a living by fishing the waters. Also, there was not much timber in the West of Ireland, and what fishing boats existed were small and fragile. People did engage in small-scale fishing, but fish remained a luxury, and potatoes were the subsistence food of fishermen. When the potato crop failed in 1847, fishermen all over Ireland pawned or sold their gear to buy meal to feed their families. Though the seas were teeming with fish, they were inaccessible to the Irish.

Phil and I found our way back to the car. A gentle mist had moved in from the Atlantic, blanketing the area with fog. With no words to describe our feelings, we drove in silence. As the scenery changed and the town of Cahersiveen emerged from the haze, we headed out towards Ballinskelligs in search of Bridget's townland.

CHAPTER 4

Ballinskelligs Bound

Storm clouds gathered overhead while the mist from the ocean spread light drops of dew on our windshield. The road narrowed, and the chilling fog rolled in. We turned up the heat. Riding along the coastline to Ballinskelligs, we got not only spectacular glimpses of the coastline through the intermittent fog, but we could also hear the mighty Atlantic Ocean force its arrival onto the rocky Kerry shores. We caught views of rugged cliffs stacked with boulders, and we watched as the thickening fog engulfed us. Phil slowed down so that we wouldn't miss the bridge that indicated the halfway point to Patrick's cottage. He carefully followed the thin strip of pavement while I wondered if we would ever find the place.

When we entered The Glen, the fog lifted. The views were so spectacular that Phil pulled the car to the side of the road so we could take it all in. I rolled my window down, and the smell of clean, crisp sea air enveloped us. Spread before us were lush green valleys, foothills dotted with sheep, and cottages with smoke twirling from their chimneys—Ballinskelligs greeted us with all of its splendor.

We looked for a yellow cottage on the side of a hill, the one that would be surrounded by trees. I was relieved to know that we would get there before dark.

We spotted Patrick's cottage tucked inside the only bushy area in The Glen. Barely able to see the color yellow, we noticed smoke rising from the chimney, and we hoped that meant Patrick was home. Phil pulled into the driveway lined with tall bushes and parked at the side of the house. A brown terrier dog barked in an attempt to look menacing, but he was too small to frighten us.

We hurried to the front door, the terrier close on our heels. The door opened and a kind gentleman smiled a warm greeting. He confirmed that it was, indeed, the cottage of Patrick O'Leary and then welcomed us inside to share the warmth of the hearth; the glow of the fire created a comfortable ambiance. Seeing we were chilled by the blustery winds, Patrick offered us a warm drink.

While enjoying the delicious tea, I couldn't help but notice how neatly he was dressed and how the flickering firelight brightened his dark eyes. He told us that he had recently retired from the Cahersiveen schools and then asked us what we did for a living. I told Patrick that I was also recently retired from teaching, and we compared experiences. Phil explained his interest in real estate, and they discussed housing prices and land values.

I then told Patrick we were searching for family—the family of a Bridget Murphy from the townland of Allaghee More in Ballinskelligs. He listened carefully as I told him about her emigration in 1880 and her life in America.

While I talked, he examined the documents. He recognized the family name and told us the Murphy family still lived in the old cottage in The Glen. Checking over the 1901 Irish Census and the Land Deeds, he announced that he did, indeed, know this family. He rattled off the names of Bridget's brothers and sisters and all of their children. I couldn't write fast enough. Patrick's enthusiasm matched ours, and I hoped that this Bridget was my grandmother.

Patrick planned to take us to the cemetery where Bridget's parents were buried and then on to the Murphy cottage in the townland of Allaghee More.

The sun would be setting soon, and it looked like it was about to storm. Patrick suggested we get started. He reminded us how dangerous the roads were during the day as well as at night and especially with the rain. Recalling our harrowing drive to his cottage, we were ready to leave in order to get it all in before dark. Grabbing our coats, we followed Patrick out the door with instructions to follow his car.

The minute Phil turned the key in the ignition, a torrential downpour flooded the gravel driveway. The rain fell in sheets; we couldn't see anything in front of us. Patrick suggested we turn around in his driveway because it was too dangerous to back onto the road, so Phil inched his way forward and then backward into the fields while squinting through the windshield to avoid the little terrier that was relentless in his pursuit of us. Meanwhile, Patrick waited patiently at the top of the driveway. After much maneuvering, we were relieved to be on our way.

Our first stop was the cemetery where Bridget's parents were buried. Just as we pulled into the centuries-old graveyard, the rain stopped as quickly as it had begun. We grabbed for our umbrellas just in case we needed them and reached for the camera before following Patrick through the entrance in search of the Murphy graves. These remains would be those of my great-grandparents, if indeed, this Bridget was my grandmother.

Patrick took us to the grave of Cornelius and Ellen (Sullivan) Murphy and two of their great-grandchildren who were buried in the same small plot. Ellen and Cornelius had died in the early 1900s; we were surprised there were four people in that one grave. Patrick told us there were probably nine deceased in that one plot. He explained that it was the custom to reuse a grave. The coffins are made of pine, and they usually rot within fifteen years. The body decomposes along with the box and when the grave is re-dug, the remains are carefully gathered and placed on top of the new pine box.

Patrick guided us into an old ruined church dating from the eleventh century. Two long, narrow windows that served as bow and arrow ports remain visible to this day. We learned that a guard had always been posted to warn of an attack from the sea. While Patrick explained the history of the structure, I couldn't help but think how fortunate we were to have found him. His knowledge of the area and its history was impressive.

The gray storm clouds returned, threatening to delay our drive to the Murphy cottage. Patrick expressed his concern about the impending storm and suggested we leave immediately. We hurried to our car and waited for Patrick to take the lead. The rain returned with a vengeance, making the narrow road more hazardous than usual. Steering the car just a little too far to the right could easily cause us to slip off the cliffs. But I felt secure with Phil at the wheel; I tried to relax and not glance over my shoulder. The wind blew the rain sideways, rocking our car with its force.

We followed Patrick, watching carefully for his brake lights. After a white-knuckle drive through The Glen, we were relieved to see his turn signal indicating our arrival at the Murphy cottage.

Just as we pulled off the main road, the rain stopped. Rays of sun streaked through gaps in the clouds, and we were able to see the lovely old cottage that was nestled at the foot of a rock-terraced pasture. The emerald green fields sparkled. Dozens of wooly sheep fed on the velvet grass. Drops of rainwater clinging to each blade of grass reflected the colors of the rainbow that suddenly appeared. Vivid purples and yellows striped the sky. We wished the time would stop so that we could slow motion our journey; I also wished for this old cottage to be the birthplace of my grandmother.

Patrick motioned for us to join him at the gate. Standing alongside him was a tall man dressed in a heavy wool jacket with a thick wool cap pulled down over his ears. We heard him tell Patrick that he saw us coming through the storm, and he wondered who would venture out in such terrible weather.

After we introduced ourselves, Patrick told the man why we were there. I then said something very foolish—I told him we were cousins. The man only glanced my way before instructing us to follow him. While walking, I thought of how much I regretted making that statement because this man had no idea who we were, and I was sure my comment would be viewed suspiciously.

We followed him through the back door of the small cottage. The minute we entered the cozy room, the warmth from the peat fire surrounded us. An old man was seated by a large picture window overlooking the pasture. He invited us to sit next to the fire. Patrick took a seat directly across from him while Phil and I found a comfortable spot on the couch.

Patrick introduced the brothers as James and Daniel Murphy. Daniel, who greeted us at the gate, had a long angular face, and I couldn't help but think that I had seen him somewhere before. His brother James, seated across from Patrick, had a round face and a light-colored complexion—not the weathered face of a farmer. Clean-shaven and neatly dressed in overalls, James looked prepared for company; he appeared relaxed and rested in contrast to Daniel, whose face was raw from the biting wind and whose hair was matted down from the weight of his cap. They both looked to be in their late seventies.

Patrick explained the reason for our visit. The brothers spoke in a thick brogue. They addressed their remarks to Patrick, glancing our way only when we spoke. I took out all the documents that I had collected for Bridget Murphy: her 1865 birth certificate, the 1880 ship records to Castle Gardens, N.Y., her marriage certificate from 1885, and her 1913 death certificate. James took each of the documents and studied them. Then he handed them to Daniel. James told Patrick that this was their Bridget Murphy from Allaghee More but that she couldn't be my grandmother.

Patrick told the brothers about the work we had done to collect all the documents. Then James told Patrick their Bridget never emigrated to America and that the only recognizable document was her birth certificate. Turning to me, Patrick asked if I had anything else that would show this Bridget Murphy to be ours. No, I had given them all I had. The only document the brothers were in agreement with was her birth certificate. The other documents they couldn't identify because their Bridget Murphy died in the cottage in this townland of Allaghee More.

Daniel told Patrick there was an Allaghee More in Killarney and thought maybe my Bridget was from another town. Not wanting to believe what I heard, I asked if they would look over my documents one more time. Patrick told me that it was no use because their Bridget was buried up in the old graveyard that we had just visited.

The Murphy brothers identified every family member who emigrated to America, going as far back as 1870. Their Bridget Murphy who was born in 1865, the one that I identified as my grandmother, never left Ireland.

The birth certificate of Bridget Murphy with the mother's maiden name Sullivan, townland of Allaghee More brought us to this place in Ballinskelligs, but it's the wrong Bridget. Patrick handed all the documents back to me. It seemed that the best thing for us to do was thank the brothers for their time, say our good-byes, and leave the Murphy cottage.

Phil and I were disappointed and exhausted. Being careful not to step in the mud, we walked single file on a narrow grass strip. I pulled the collar of my jacket up around my face to protect myself from the gusty winds.

Patrick followed close behind. We thanked him for his help, for without him, we wouldn't have met the Murphy family, and we would have assumed this place to be the birthplace of my grandmother.

Backing down the long narrow driveway, we decided that the search for the other Bridget Murphy from the townland of Ballyhearney would have to wait for another day. It was dark and the roads were dangerous. We had followed the trail of this Bridget all the way to the cottage where she was born, and we even met her family. That was quite an accomplishment, and we felt confident we could also find the Bridget Murphy from Ballyhearney. But not on this trip, for we leave for home tomorrow.

Night skies were further blackened by the storm clouds, and the roads were flooded from the recent downpour. The beams of our headlights scattered the fog, making it difficult to see. The roads were so narrow in this area that we wondered how in the world the oncoming traffic would be able to pass us. Luckily, we didn't have to worry about that as we had the road to ourselves all the way back to Cahersiveen.

We decided to eat dinner at one of the pubs in town. It was late and fatigue dulled our spirits; a good hot meal would serve us well. Our dinner conversation focused on the Murphy brothers. I remembered why Daniel looked so familiar; he resembled my father's brother Frank. I remembered from the pictures that my cousin had sent me. The Murphy brothers could be distant relatives of my Murphy family, but that seemed like a long shot. Besides, our mission was to find the birthplace of my grandmother. If we were lucky enough to find any relatives, we would consider that a bonus.

When we returned to our room, I pulled out all the information on the other Bridget from Valentia Island. This must be our Bridget, the one whose mother's maiden name was Connor.

Today's discovery had provided another piece to the puzzle. When we visited Bridget's grave in Omaha, Nebraska, her gravestone inscription indicated that she was born in Valentia. So, rather than being disappointed, we were encouraged to know that my Bridget is most likely the one from the townland of Ballyhearney.

We wished we could stay longer in Ireland, but it wasn't possible. We hoped to return within six months, for this would give us enough time to dig a little deeper to see what we could find on Bridget from Ballyhearney in Valentia. Following the lead on the mother's maiden name of Connor would require some proof, for what proof did we have? And we still didn't know much about my grandfather Michael's life in Ireland, only that he was born on Carhan Lower. It appears we had just scratched the surface.

CHAPTER 5

Enchanted Valentia

May 2004

Our return to Ireland found us back at the cottage of Patrick O'Leary. On this day we weren't running to escape the rain and winds but rather taking time to enjoy the magnificent view from Patrick's front yard. The rolling sea crashed into quiet waters, reflecting deep blues richly tinted with the bright hue of polished turquoise. White foam washed over huge rocks while graceful seagulls screeched their delight in nature's bountiful playground. Waves pounded the cliffs, scattering ocean spray on the fertile pastures. Curious fluffy white sheep watched as we walked up the path to Patrick's cottage. Hedge clippers tossed on top of an uneven hedge gave us the impression that Patrick might not be enjoying his retirement from the Cahersiveen schools as much as he had hoped.

His small barking dog alerted him of our arrival; he greeted us at the door while bandaging his arm. Apparently, two large dogs had bitten him while he was protecting his own dog. Seeing our concern, he assured us that he was fine. He invited us inside and left to prepare the tea.

In his tidy parlor, the curtains were pulled back, and sun filtered through the windows. Dust particles floated on the sunbeams and settled into the carpet.

Patrick entered the sitting room carrying a silver tray filled with lovely china cups; the soothing aroma of tea surrounded us. He told us that he had recently visited the Murphy Brothers on Ballinskelligs, and that they asked about our search for Bridget. The subject reminded me of our former disappointment, but I showed Patrick the birth certificate that I brought for a Bridget Murphy born on Valentia Island in the townland of Ballyhearney. He scrutinized the document, then cautioned us that there were many Murphy families on Valentia. He suggested we visit the Valentia Heritage Center Museum for information and told us to stop at the Ring Lyne Pub in Chapeltown to talk with John Francis O'Sullivan, a well-known Valentia historian.

We chatted about the weather, his children, and the two big dogs that had recently taken up residence next door. We finished our tea and thanked Patrick for his help. Walking to the car, I chided him about his half-clipped hedge. Amused, he assured us that on our next visit we would find those clippers in the very same place. He then pointed us in the direction of Portmagee, telling us to watch for the bridge that would take us into Valentia.

After a few miles of winding road, the fishing village of Portmagee came into view. From Portmagee we spotted Valentia, a beautiful island resting alongside Ireland. A bridge constructed in 1970 connects Valentia to Ireland. When my grandmother emigrated in 1880 there were 2,000 residents on Valentia, but, today, only 600 people remain.

I recently learned that Valentia Island is seven miles long and three miles wide and that it lies in the Gulf Stream. The beauty of its rich and colorful landscape didn't escape us on our drive through Chapeltown. Wild rhododendrons compete with the trees, while ferns and palms wave in the gentle breeze. The goldfinch and robins bring a dazzling show of color and the tiny wren defends its territory with song. Entering the small village of Knightstown, we looked carefully for the museum.

We were surprised to see such a small building. Tucked away and squeezed between two very old structures, it appeared insignificant. A sign at the entrance informed the visitor about the treasured memorabilia from the Trans-Atlantic Cable laid in 1858. For over one hundred years, the cable was an important part of life on Valentia Island. Not only did the island become the end of the line in Europe but also, in the early years, every message crossing the Atlantic passed through the station at Valentia. Emigration records and old school files had been preserved at the Heritage Center as well.

We had an hour before it opened. Across the road was a centuries-old church, and our curiosity motivated us to investigate. The old brick building, blackened with age, showed signs of decay. Original stained glass windows provided the only beauty to its ugly façade. Thorny weeds wound their way through the cracks, creating shadows on the inside walls. Two towering oak trees shaded the church, waving their branches in the breeze as if to resuscitate the old building. This Protestant Church closed when the English landlords left the island in the early 1900s. Although the Protestant population grew with the building of the cable in the middle 1800s, there remain today only three Protestant families on Valentia.

We noticed a red truck parked alongside our car, and, concerned that perhaps we were parked illegally, we approached the driver. A white-haired, rosy-cheeked woman speaking in a very thick brogue asked if we needed help. We told her about our search for the Murphy family and how we were now waiting for the museum to open. She said she knew a man named Sean whose mother was a Murphy, and she thought he might know something about my Murphy family, so she instructed us to follow her car.

Taking the Low Road, we arrived at Sean's cottage in minutes. Not sure if he would speak with us, she asked us to wait in the car, then turned and disappeared into his weed-infested yard. Meanwhile, an elderly gentleman dressed in a three-piece suit approached us. Surprised by his sudden appearance, we introduced ourselves. At that same moment, Sean appeared at his gate.

Sean's fingernails were caked with dirt and his clothes soiled with grease. He approached me with a scowl on his prickly, unshaven face and asked what made me think I was Irish. Surprised at the outburst, I told him that I was as Irish as he was because all four of my grandparents were born in Ireland. He asked to see the papers I carried in my briefcase. I located Bridget's birth certificate and pulled it from my satchel. Sean and the old gentleman consulted with each other. The two old men rattled on about the Murphy families in the area, drawing the conclusion that I was not in any way connected to them because their relations never lived on Ballyhearney. I was relieved not to be related to Sean. We thanked both men for their time and headed for the museum.

When we arrived at the museum, we were delighted to see that it was open. We paid the Two Euro entry fee and began our self-tour of Valentia's past, reading with interest the 1875 Corporal Punishment Book from the Ballyhearney School. Students who were late in the morning, disobedient, careless, caught telling untruths or scratching other children warranted a whack with the cane across their hands. I wondered if my grandmother ever suffered such punishment.

I approached the volunteer on duty. Busy filing information, he turned carefully while reaching for his crutch; he told us he was recovering from hip replacement surgery. At eighty-six, he looked fit and said he was happy to be back at work. I showed him the 1870 Land Deed from Ballyhearney and Bridget's birth certificate from 1865. He commented on the many Murphy families on the island and said that my Bridget could belong to any one of them. Just then I remembered before leaving home, I had tucked an old letter into my briefcase. Mailed from Ireland in 1949, the letter was addressed to my cousin Mary in Spokane, Washington. Mary sent it to me just recently, thinking it might help in my search. The letter was from our cousin Hannah Keating. It read:

CoarhaBeg
Sept. 13, 1949

My Dear Cousin Mary:

I received your long looked for letter yesterday. I was delighted to hear from you, but sorry to hear about all your illness. I'm not so well in health all the time, but not so bad either. People must put up with everything that comes their way.

I was looking forward for a letter from you or your mother all this time. I sent you some books, did you get them? I hope you did. I would be very thankful if you would send me a package of clothes. I mean things that you would not want as they would be most useful to us here.

My brother's name is John. He is 45 years old and is not married. He does his own work, which is very hard. I could have helped him a little now only I took ill myself after the death of my father and Aunt Kate.

We had a most beautiful year, fine weather all the year, only today is raining. Could you ever send me a few snaps of yourself and your brothers and sisters. I would love also to get a picture of your father and mother. I have no pictures of myself that I could send, but perhaps I could send you a few snaps later on.

Will you please send this to me and send me snaps as I'd surely love to see your picture.

I must finish hoping to hear from you soon. Love and best wishes to allxxxx

From Hannah
To Cousin Mary

It took only a moment for him to identify the writer. He remembered Hannah. She passed away in 1985. I looked more closely at the postmark but couldn't read it, as half was torn away from the envelope. He identified the letter as being mailed from Cahersiveen and the townland of CoarhaBeg was up the road. Then he said that Hannah's maiden name was Connor and that her mother was a Murphy.

Everything appeared as if in slow motion, and a rush of heat flooded my face. I heard a buzzing sound and felt myself sway. Phil, noticing my distress, wrapped his arms around me. I leaned into him, grateful for his support.

Hannah's letter had returned to Ireland after fifty-five years. Yellowed with age, frayed and torn, it provided the missing piece to our family puzzle. Hannah Keating and Bridget Murphy were related; they shared the same family name of Connor, but how were they related? We asked where the Catholic cemetery was located. We thought Hannah might be buried in a plot near the Murphy family. Leaning on his crutches, the clerk wrote directions to the Kylemore Burial Grounds. We thanked him for his valuable help and left in search of Hannah's grave.

Driving off the main road onto an unpaved one, we followed the signs to the Kylemore Graveyard and turned into the small parking area. Two women got out of their car at the same time we did, so we followed them. The graveyard was terraced; it looked as though the older graves were at the top. I walked towards them while Phil agreed to search the middle and bottom terraces. A few minutes later, I looked up to see Phil waving for me to join him. I approached quietly because he was engrossed in a serious conversation with one of the women. Phil introduced me to my cousin, Kathleen Corless. Her maiden name is Murphy; she was also Hannah's cousin.

Amazed to meet a cousin in of all places a cemetery, I showed her Hannah's letter. While we attempted to figure out where I stood on the cousin chain, Phil compared the shape of our ears, and Kathleen's friend noticed our same-shaped noses. We learned that Kathleen's husband had recently died, and she was visiting his grave. A difficult day for Kathleen, but I was cheered by meeting family.

She had no information on my Bridget, nor did she know where my grandmother fit in the family. She suggested that we talk to one of Hannah's old school chums, Eileen Tierney, who she thought would know about Hannah's relatives. The woman with Kathleen introduced herself as Patsy Murphy—we were meeting so many Murphy families—but Kathleen assured us that Patsy was not related to the Murphys from Ballyhearney.

Since the two women would drive past Eileen's cottage on their way home, we were told to follow them that far. Before getting into her car, Patsy wrote directions to her place. She wanted to see us after our visit with Eileen; in fact, she insisted we come that afternoon.

Patsy had told us that Eileen Tierney, at ninety-one, had the distinction of being the oldest person living on Valentia. She lived alone in her three-room cottage surrounded by the farm worked by her son. Only one of her ten children stayed to care for Eileen. Our loud knock brought her to the door. Eileen invited us inside, asking our names as she shuffled to her hard-backed, wooden chair. Her silver white hair, pulled up in a braided bun, framed a full face. An apron, spotted and worn, hung loosely over her flowered print dress.

The story of Bridget and Hannah unfolded. I told Eileen about meeting Kathleen in the cemetery while I looked for Hannah's grave. I asked if she knew anything about Hannah that could help in our search for Bridget. She told us that she and Hannah had been childhood friends and that Hannah had married Lawrence Keating; they had no children.

I showed her the letter from Hannah. Eileen asked me to read it. While I unfolded the letter, she held a lace-trimmed handkerchief to her eyes. A gentle smile spread across her face as I slowly read. When I finished, she reached to take the letter from my hand and placed it on the table in front of her. She identified Hannah's Aunt Kate as her aunt, as well, married to her uncle. I mentioned Hannah's letter returning to Ireland after fifty-five years and how we were now searching for facts about her, hoping to find information about Bridget. Unfortunately, Eileen couldn't tell us anything about Hannah's family.

She offered us tea, but we declined. It looked as though she had just enough for herself in the little tea box on the shelf. The kettle sat on top of an iron peat stove shoved into the hearth. She related her dislike of cooking on the iron stove; she missed her large hearth fireplace with the pots that hung from an iron rod. Eileen recalled that everything tasted better when cooked in the heavy cast-iron pots.

She was grateful for our company and told us stories about her difficult life on the farm. When her children were small, she said she awoke before dawn to tend the fire, baked bread, and cooked porridge. She worked in the fields alongside her husband, digging turf, milking cows, slaughtering the pig, and churning the butter. There was no electricity—it didn't come to the island until 1959— nor was there indoor plumbing. Water was carried in heavy wooden buckets from a well shared by three families. She told us a family required two acres of potatoes to feed themselves and their pig to get through the year.

When she was a young girl, life was even harder. There was little light after darkness fell. Paraffin oil came on the market in the 1940's and was burned in small hand lamps. Before paraffin, her family boiled fish oil and burned it in a scallop shell with dry peeled rushes for wicks. If fat was available, they would dissolve tallow using cotton thread for wicks— homemade candles. Another source of light was bogwood cut into long splinters. Someone in the family would hold lighted splinters for the women spinning wool. Eileen remembered how she and Hannah held splinters for hours.

Boots were a luxury, to be worn to church services and in the winter when frost covered the ground. She remembered her father slaughtering newborn calves and peeling away their skin for tanning. The calf hides provided the softest leather for shoes and boots, which could be sold at the markets. Her family would wear none of these shoes and boots. They brought good money, and they needed every shilling they could earn.

When her children were growing up, neighbors gathered in the evenings around Eileen's hearth to share gossip, sew garments, and knit sweaters and socks. Wool was prepared and dyed at home. First, the sheep were washed in the river and left to dry for a couple of days. Then they were sheared and the wool was combed and oiled by hand. Black dye was produced from the mud at the bottom of the bog. Leaves of ragwort were used to make the color brown, while heather and fuchsia flowers produced colors woven into shepherd's plaid. Human urine set the colors. During the dying period it was important not to eat cabbage or turnips, as that would affect the quality of the urine used.

Completely self-sufficient, Eileen spoke proudly of her family's ability to survive, relying on no one outside of their small community. The cow was brought in at night to supply heat to warm the cottage. It was not unusual to see the pigs, cows, and chickens sharing Eileen's hearth. A large wooden barrel stood in the corner; it held the salted carcass of the pig.

Irish wasn't taught in the National School, but it was the home language. She said her parents knew very little English. She went to school with a breakfast of dry bread and oatmeal gruel boiled in a skillet on an open turf fire. It was her only nourishment until dinner. Farmers' children had no butter or jam for their bread. They had to sell their butter and eggs to pay the rent to the landlord, or be evicted. Children went to school barefoot. As poor as they were, each student was expected to bring a sod of turf to school to make a fire.

Eileen treated us to a tour of her cottage. The room in back of the hearth was her sitting room. Small and cozy, its wide windowsills held pictures and dusty vases of dried flowers. A threadbare carpet fringed with oyster colored strings showed evidence of past bright hues. The walls, painted moss green, were peeling from the moisture that had settled into the room. Magazines and newspapers were stacked next to a basket of knitting. The kitchen jutted out from the side of the house, an addition made in the last fifty years. A modern sink with a small refrigerator and tiny cooking stove looked well used. A huge picture window allowed Eileen a magnificent view of the Atlantic Ocean. This part of Ireland is scenically spectacular, with mountains sweeping sharply up to meet the ever-changing sky, while tiny green valleys filled with pink primroses and yellow buttercups lie tucked away. We were hypnotized by the view. Eileen interrupted our trance to show us her new washing machine. She enjoyed the conveniences of the twenty-first century, remembering days spent scrubbing clothes on a washboard and draping them over the bushes to dry. We thanked Eileen for her hospitality. She stood at her cottage door waving, as our car climbed to the top of the gravel driveway.

Our next stop was Patsy's yellow cottage, which sat beside a washed-out dirt path. A vegetable garden bordered her front walk. We wondered how anything could grow here; the rocky ground looked forbidding to all plant life.

Patsy, a stocky woman with dark hair and a warm smile, waved a welcome from her doorway. She climbed into our car and directed us slowly up the gravel path towards Hannah's cottage and St. Brendan's Holy Well. Phil carefully maneuvered the car on the deeply rutted mud road. The car leaned into the fields and dipped into the deep crevices. Patsy apologized for the poor condition of the road, saying that even though the Kerry Council had voted to repair it, she didn't know when they would schedule it. Unfortunately, this was the only way to get to where we were going.

St. Brendan's was located in the middle of a bog. We walked on the black rubber mats that were planted across the field and teetered on the narrow strip of lumber in order to ensure our safety. Patsy cautioned us not to step into the bog, but curiosity got the best of me. I lowered my foot into the bog water, thinking it would settle on ground, but it didn't. My foot disappeared in the muck. Patsy reprimanded me and told us that many small animals fell into the bog and died.

She explained that Sunday Mass was often celebrated in the summer months at St. Brendan's Holy Well. The faithful circled the shrine, praying the Rosary. After prayers, the penitents used a small stone to scratch the sign of the cross into the granite slab. Visitors left statues and small doll parts, which symbolized their wishes: a head could represent prayers for headache relief, a foot for bunions, and so forth.

It was important to see Hannah and Lawrence Keating's cottage; we appreciated Patsy going with us, for we would never have found the place without her help. Abandoned, this 300-year-old cottage stood strong against the wind. Stones of various sizes, stacked with sand to cement them together, formed the walls. Tiny windows, caked with salt from the sea, offered us a glance into the past. A wooden barrel pushed up against the wall once stored the butchered, salted pig. A large open-hearth fireplace, empty of peat, loomed vacant and cold. Whitewashed stonewalls flecked by eroding rock separated the rooms.

Patsy told us stories of a decayed marriage embittered further by Hannah's inability to conceive a child. Convinced she was dying of breast cancer, Hannah lived the last twenty years as a recluse, refusing to listen to the doctor or open her door to neighbors. Unrelenting hardships, poverty and anguish set the stage for a lifetime of unhappiness.

The pastures surrounding Hannah's cottage were rich with peat that provided fuel for the locals. As a young woman, Hannah would dig turf, load it on donkey carts, and haul it into town to sell. Located a few hundred yards from the rocky Atlantic Coast, her cottage stood like a barren oak tree in a fifty-acre field.

I visualize a young Hannah walking away from the cottage in the year 1949; she carries a letter to her family in America, asking for clothes and snapshots. She carries her letter carefully, protecting it from the wind that gusts around her.

Dark pink sea holly creeps up the rocks to join the bog pimpernel in a carpet of pastels, dotted with the blooming white puffs of bog cotton. Seagulls floating on wind currents glide overhead, an oil-canvassed landscape. In the distance are beautifully colored flowers, but not one was ever brave enough to move towards Hannah's cottage. I was convinced that surviving on this land surpassed any experience imaginable, and my thoughts drifted to my grandmother Bridget. She had stood here; she must have. Her young eyes rested on every rock I see. Her dreams were gathered in the waving field grasses, and they continue to soar in every wind current. A wildflower drifted past me, and for a moment I felt Bridget's presence.

I thought about what I recently learned about Irish emigration in the year 1880, the year Bridget left home. British landlords believed that emigration was an alternative to eviction and that it would solve Ireland's population problem. The cost of emigration for a pauper was about half the cost of maintaining him in the workhouse for one year, and once the ship sailed, the landlord was rid of the problem. Burial across the sea in strange lands away from loved ones seemed a cruel punishment for the crime of being born Irish.

Patsy told us about the "Cap" Murphys. They lived across the channel in Portmagee. She was sure that John "Cap" and Hannah were related. I asked what "Cap" meant. Patsy laughed and explained that so many Murphys live on Valentia that the townspeople had to give them nicknames. There is a "Paris" Murphy because he lives in the townland of Paris. A "Clerk" Murphy identified the parish clerk, and "Pirate" Murphy was derived from a legend of the sea. The "Cap" Murphys wore a particular kind of sealskin cap that distinguished them from the others. Then Patsy handed me John "Cap's" phone number, along with directions to his cottage. Promising to write to her, we climbed into our car to leave. She wished us God speed and continued to wave as we rounded the corner.

It was six o'clock; four hours of daylight remained. Exhausted from the day's events, we decided to find some good pub food and turn in early. Tomorrow would be a good day to visit John "Cap" Murphy. I couldn't believe our luck at having located another family member, but I wondered whether or not John had any information; after all, Bridget had left Valentia one hundred and twenty-four years ago.

The next morning promised a beautiful day. While enjoying a delicious Irish breakfast of bacon, eggs, homemade brown bread, and tea, we watched the sun rise slowly into a clear blue sky. A few clouds lingered before drifting off in the direction of Dublin. Our view was spectacular! Tucked into the valley surrounded by gently sloping pastures, a few farms graced the landscape. White, velvet feathered Gannets circled in groups overhead, searching for breakfast. They plunged into the sea in pursuit of their feast. Satisfied, they settled on the rocks to preen their feathers. The beautiful birds with orange webbed feet and golden heads chatted noisily to one another while gathering for their bird dance. Choughs flew overhead, spirited by the lively chirping of the Gannets.

We discussed our plans for the day. After two years of searching birth records, spending hours mulling over the microfilms in the Family History Library in Salt Lake City, and collecting family information from my cousins in America, we were close to finding Bridget's family. The anticipation lifted my spirits. I practiced what I would say when I was introduced to John "Cap." After my encounter with the Murphy brothers in Ballinskelligs, I didn't want to scare this man. Phil and I rehearsed how and what I should say because it was important not to overwhelm John with my enthusiasm and any assumption of a relationship to his family.

It was only a short drive to the seaside village of Portmagee, and we had time to stop for a cup of tea. I couldn't remember when I had felt so nervous. I am about to meet family members, and I was hoping they would be happy to see us. The hot tea soothed my jitters. Phil and I sat watching people gather on this beautiful Saturday morning. We lingered, afraid and excited at the same time. Our teapots were empty, and we noticed family groups waiting for seats; it was time for us to leave the security of our table.

Patsy had provided excellent directions. After passing a grotto, we spotted the stacks of peat she had told us would be piled alongside the road. We were looking for a house on the corner where we were to make a right turn. My heart raced! The winding road provided a welcome distraction from the butterflies in my stomach.

We pulled into John's driveway and parked in front of a lovely dwelling. A tall stone fence surrounded the tidy remodeled vintage-cottage. Lace curtains hung at the windows, and a welcome mat rested on the stoop by a new front door. A small brown dog barking loudly ran to meet us. My eyes were focused on the front door.

The door opened and a woman stood in front of me. I was at a complete loss for words. I would have preferred being lifted by the errant gulls flying overhead and dropped into the sea rather than standing at this door. The startled look on my face caused her to step back. I asked if a John "Cap" lived there. She said yes and asked our business with him. I knew better than to hint at our relationship; however, I told her that I was related to Hannah, which would mean I was a relation of John. That sentence rolled out; I didn't mean it to. I must have looked uncomfortable, for she introduced herself as John's wife, Kitty, and invited us inside.

Kitty was tall with a beautiful figure. Curly salt and pepper hair framed her lovely features. She was radiant, wearing very little make-up with just a touch of lipstick. Her flowered dress was neatly pressed; she was wearing red shoes. Kitty looked dressed for an occasion, and I was hoping that occasion would be this family reunion.

John was busy in the back of the house. When he entered the room, Kitty made introductions. He was wearing an old shirt tucked into a pair of soiled work pants. After a good, firm handshake, he excused himself. Kitty offered tea and we accepted. She brought out her finest china and silver, and a variety of delicious cakes and breads. We heard boiling water rumbling against the sides of an aluminum teakettle.

While she set the table, Kitty asked about our trip. We told her about meeting Kathleen in the cemetery and how

Patsy Murphy had sent us to their cottage. When we told her we had traveled from Chicago, she said she had worked as a nurse in New York City for three years back in the 1950s.

We admired their furnishings and the view from the large picture window that overlooked the harbor. I noticed a lovely old buffet cabinet; Kitty informed us that it had belonged to her mother. A large iron peat stove blazed with turf, while cakes and biscuits cooled on the iron grates. The cottage smelled welcoming, somewhat easing my fears.

John returned to the parlor wearing suit trousers and a dress shirt. He sat down beside me and asked why I had come. For an awful moment, my anxiety returned. I dug around in my bag for the letter from Hannah. There was so much to say, and I didn't know where to begin. When John heard I was from Chicago, he told me his people had emigrated to New London, Connecticut. I told him that Bridget had emigrated to Connecticut in 1880 and was married in Norwich/New London in 1885. John listened with renewed interest. He reached for Hannah's letter. After reading it, he passed it to Kitty. She read with interest, then carefully placed it on the table. There was no doubt the letter was from John's cousin, Hannah.

We have found the family of my grandmother Bridget Murphy!

I told John I had received Hannah's letter from my cousin Mary, who lives in Washington. Silence hung thick in the air as John took one document after the other and studied them: Bridget's birth certificate, ship record, marriage certificate, pictures of Bridget's children (including my father), and Bridget's death certificate. John told me his grandmother was born in the townland of Ballyhearney in 1858. He could see by the birth certificate that my grandmother was born in the same townland in the year 1865. Our grandmothers were sisters! John didn't recall his grandmother, Mary, ever talking about a sister named Bridget. We spoke of sad partings when family members left for America. Bridget knew she would never see her family again. John explained we were from the "Clerk" Murphys because our grandmothers' brother had worked as the clerk in the church in Chapeltown, Valentia. John was a "Cap" Murphy because of the sealskin cap his father wore. When we told them about meeting Kathleen Corless, they told us that Kathleen's grandfather was my grandmother's brother.

How wonderful to be sitting in a cottage in Ireland conversing with my cousins, John and Kitty Murphy! Kitty rushed from the room to look for pictures of Hannah while John talked about his life in Ireland. We were surprised to learn that he was actually born in Boston in 1928. His parents returned to Ireland when he was one year old. John told us about the hardships of growing up in Ireland in the 1930s, as Ireland didn't recover from the Depression as quickly as the rest of the world. He had often wondered what his life would have been like had his parents stayed in Boston.

Kitty returned and apologized for not being able to locate any pictures of Hannah, but she promised to look further and mail them to me. Pictures stacked on the credenza caught my eye. John and Kitty told us about each of their nine children, who were now grown and had families of their own.

Our time spent with John and Kitty included conversations about family, and they shared stories about the wonderful events in their lives. They were truly blessed with not only a beautiful family but with each other as well. With Kitty's delicious cakes, we celebrated our return to Ballyhearney and to the family Bridget never knew.

It was settled! I was a cousin, and there was no need to further search the documents for proof of that. Hannah's letter had cinched it.

We had kept them long enough; it was time to pack away my papers and say good-bye. We posed for photos and promised to write. John reached for my hand as we walked to the gate. Looking across the harbor, he pointed to Ballyhearney, identifying that townland as our home— the place of our ancestors! I was satisfied; I belonged to that island. Kitty blessed us with the holy water stored in her front hall and wished us a safe journey.

I was overjoyed to have found family but also saddened by Bridget's loss. She never told my father or any of her children about her life in Ireland. The sorrow she carried in her heart for Ballyhearney and the family she left behind must have filled her with an overwhelming grief for all of her life.

I will remember our journey as one of the most wonderful moments in my life. I had always wondered about my father's family. Maybe learning about the life of my grandmother will help me to understand the sadness my father carried in his heart.

CHAPTER 6

Ballyhearney

We awoke to the aroma of frying bacon. The crows screeched their morning greeting as we stretched and kicked back the covers. We had slept later than usual and now, remembering that we needed to meet John Francis O'Sullivan after the eleven o'clock Mass, we dressed, ate breakfast, and hurried out the door.

Blue skies glistened overhead while the early morning sun burned off the fog that lingered in the valleys; the coastline was bright with new patches of sea pinks. The valleys, carpeted in yellow irises with drifts of bluebells and wildflowers, offered fragrances that mingled with crisp ocean air.

Today, we were going to visit the townland of Ballyhearney—the birthplace of my grandmother. But first, it was important that we attend Mass at the St. Derarca and St. Teresa Church in Chapeltown. Driving along the coast and through the village of Portmagee, I noticed the small teashop that we had stopped in before our visit with John and Kitty. Yesterday, I anguished about finding my Murphy family. Today, I was completely satisfied and grateful to have found cousins.

We followed the main road to the bridge built in 1970 that connected Valentia with Portmagee. It opened the world to the island residents, for it was no longer necessary for a doctor to reside on the island, and people could visit friends and relatives any time they liked. Meetings were no longer limited to the big city fairs, and the residents of Portmagee could enjoy an evening in one of the charming Valentia pubs. Even though Valentia has lost its isolation, it continues to successfully maintain its identity as an island.

We made a right turn off the bridge onto the Low road that would take us into Chapeltown and arrived just as the priest was getting out of his car. Before rushing into church, he commented on the windy day we brought with us from America. Our visit must be news on the island.

The small-whitewashed chapel, adorned with jeweled stained glass windows, was built in 1939, replacing the old church built in 1829. A short wooden cross stuck out from the top of the belfry. An old brass bell suspended by a thick gauge chain barely moved against the swift wind that was blowing off the ocean. Tombstones dating from the 1800s were scattered throughout the churchyard. Unsightly, brown-colored moss cloaked the stone fence surrounding the dismal graveyard. We followed a gravel walkway to the entrance.

The old wooden entry door had over-sized brass hinges with a brightly polished door latch that reflected the sun-rays and was warm to the touch. The door looked as though it had been rescued from the old church; its wood was richly grained and pocked from burrowing insects, and it stood strong against the brutal forces of Ireland's inclement weather.

We hurried inside as the wind gusted. The floor creaked under our weight. I envisioned a young Bridget Murphy entering the old church in 1880 to pray for a safe journey across the ocean. Despite the hardships, her faith had remained strong.

The sun filtered through the stained glass windows and provided a warm glow against the stark backdrop of the stucco walls. The air was thick with moisture. Shivering from the dampness, I hugged myself for warmth and hoped the service would be short.

The Mass was scheduled to begin in ten minutes, but Phil and I were the only people in the church. Just as we checked our watches, the doors creaked open. Footsteps pounded the wooden floor and echoed through the small chapel. The faithful filed in, filling all the back pews, while the front remained empty. When the back pews were filled, the parishioners lined up against the back wall. Places close to the door were at a premium. We heard there was a Gaelic Football game scheduled in Cahersiveen at noon, and it was our guess that the back of the church would begin to empty out long before the Mass was over. Football in Ireland takes second place only to God.

We recognized one of the women who entered the church. It was Eileen Tierney, whose cottage we had visited two days ago. Heads turned when she walked up the aisle. She carried herself like royalty and nodded a greeting to everyone. A hand-crocheted ivory shawl was draped over her lavender-pink dress and a wide brimmed straw hat circled with colorful spring flowers hid her braided hair. As if on cue, Mass began the moment she settled into her pew.

A middle-aged woman who sat next to us leaned forward and asked if we were the Americans looking for a Murphy family. She winked and said we could talk after Mass.

I thought about my grandmother Bridget and wondered what her life must have been like in this town. The families sitting around us represented generations of island residents. Their grandparents knew my grandmother. Glancing at the parishioners, I noticed their complexions were ruddy and weathered from the harsh winds. Thick, muscled hands held prayer books, and rosary beads dangled from their unmanicured fingers. This wasn't a parish rich with luxuries but rather one of hard-working people. I envied their lives so rich in tradition and old world values.

A breeze blew in from the open door. It was crisp and smelled clean, but it was chilling. Some of the men were wearing heavy woolen sweaters and warm wool caps. Wishing I had packed a wool sweater for this occasion, I inched closer to Phil for warmth.

After Mass, we joined the crowd outside. It was a Murphy who had sat next to us in church, and her entire family now circled us. Phil and I were enjoying the celebrity status bestowed upon us by the Murphys. I told them we had found our Murphy family and explained that I belonged to the "Clerk" Murphys, and I am a cousin of John "Cap." They were happy our search ended successfully. We told them about Hannah's letter and how that had led us to our family. They all remembered Hannah and expressed regret that we hadn't come sooner because we could have met her. Everybody had a story about the many Murphy families on Valentia. We listened carefully, delighting in their lilting Irish brogue. With so many Murphy families, we were, indeed, fortunate to have found ours.

We asked the ladies if they could direct us to John Francis O'Sullivan at the Ring Lyne Pub. As if out of nowhere, John appeared in the crowd. When we asked if he could spare a few moments to talk with us about the island, he instructed us to meet him in his pub in about an hour, as he had some paperwork to finish first. I remarked to one of the women how handsome he was and it was then I learned that John was eighty-five years old. He looked amazingly fit for a man that age; his fair skin was wrinkle free and his blue eyes sparkled.

I asked the ladies if they knew of a townland called Ballyhearney. There just happened to be a Bridie Murphy from Ballyhearney in the crowd. She told us her husband was also related to my Murphy family. We had found another cousin! Her husband was probably a third cousin. Bridie was married to Brendie Murphy and they lived in a newer house on Ballyhearney. I asked her if we could visit the townland; she instructed us to follow her car.

Just minutes down the road from the church, we stopped at the Murphy property gate. It would be easier to walk, as the weeds and brambles had grown onto the gravel path. Bridie told us to stay as long as we wanted. Grateful, we turned to walk the land. The original cottage had been gone since 1925. It was leveled many years after the deaths of Bridget's parents—her mother, Mary, died at the age of seventy-nine on October 12, 1912, and her father, John, passed away on August 6, 1916, at the age of ninety-three. A two-story stone house, now vacant, had replaced their old cottage. Weeds and brambles blocked the entryway and had taken root in the cracks and crevices of the old place.

Remembering our conversation from yesterday, John "Cap" said that in 1865, Bridget and her family had lived in a three-room cottage with a loft. A thatched roof with a poorly vented chimney made the air inside the cottage smoky and damp. A big hearth stone fireplace took up one wall, with two hobs built in for seating. Stone and dirt were packed together to create the floor. A wooden table was pushed up against the wall under a small window. A rack bench for extra seating leaned against the wall opposite the hearth. Bridget's parents, my great-grandparents, John and Mary Murphy and their children: John, Michael, Ellen, Kate, Bridget, Pats, Mary, and Julia lived in the crowded little cottage tucked in a meadow near the channel of Portmagee on the townland of Ballyhearney.

The cottage was no longer there, but farm equipment and fertilizer were stored in concrete block buildings that had been recently constructed. Rocky soil weighted with moss and weeds made it difficult to see the place where the cottage had stood over one hundred years ago. Although it was reassuring to know the Murphy family still owned the land, I was disappointed the cottage was gone.

We walked towards the sound of waves breaking on the shore. Ballyhearney was located directly across the channel from Ireland's mainland and the village of Portmagee. The winds were not as harsh on this channel side of Valentia, in stark contrast to Hannah's land, which was pounded by strong wind gusts off the Atlantic. Here, on Ballyhearney, gentle breezes rolled across the tall weeds. We spotted John "Cap's" place across the channel. Smoke swirled from the chimney, and we could almost smell the wonderful aroma of Kitty's biscuits.

Looking across the channel to Portmagee, we saw sand particles that sparkled like diamonds in the sunlight. But behind us on Ballyhearney prickly thorn-bushes grew, surrounded by nettles and dandelions. Tall brown grasses mixed with weeds and thistles spread like a thorny carpet over rocks and stones. Bridget's birthplace resembled an untended graveyard. A cloud drifted overhead. I felt a chill and for a moment wondered if the sadness of Bridget's departure on that spring morning in 1880 still lingered. I wondered how my grandmother had prepared herself for the long, arduous journey to America, for it must have been difficult to say good-bye to loved ones; she was only fifteen.

Turning away from the shore, we carefully followed the path that Bridget walked when she left for America. We discussed the items she was allowed to carry with her: pots, spoons, cups, two dresses, one pair of boots, a comb, brush, corn meal, and oatmeal cakes. Did she think those few things would be enough to make her life comfortable, once she settled in America? I wondered how many family members traveled with her. And was there someone waiting for her when she arrived at Castle Gardens in New York harbor? There were so many unanswered questions. Walking away from Ballyhearney, I listened carefully to the sounds my shoes made on the gravel path and wondered if Bridget heard the same sounds when she walked this path.

The Ballyhearney School, built in 1875, was located a short distance from Bridget's cottage. When Bridget was young, school wasn't mandatory because there was too much work to be done on the farm. She also worked as a servant in the Royal Hotel in Knightstown; servant girls on Valentia were taught excellent domestic skills, and those skills served Bridget well in her adopted land.

We were scheduled to meet John Francis at the Ring Lyne Pub across from the church, so we headed in that direction. It felt good to be seated in our comfortable car and out of the harsh winds.

Passing the church in Chapeltown, we saw The Ring Lyne on the left side of the road. Picnic tables were scattered around the gravel parking lot, and a handful of patrons were enjoying their glasses of beer under the sun-drenched sky. An old nondescript building, the Ring Lyne deceived the casual observer. Rugged on the outside, the inside was charming. Tables placed underneath six-paneled windows were large and looked sturdy. A big hearth fireplace flickered in the distance, adding warmth and ambiance to the lovely old pub. Pictures and vintage-posters were tacked to the walls, and the bar stretched the entire length of the long room. Stacked against a huge mirror were colorful varieties of assorted liquors. French doors separated the bar from a banquet room that was next to a full service kitchen. There was a small hotel lobby in the back because the Ring Lyne was also a hostel. A crowd was expected after the football game, so we were grateful for any time that John would give us.

We asked the barkeeper if John was available. She told us he was out walking his dog Rambo but was expected back at any moment. We ordered a couple of cold drinks and located seats close to the fire.

John entered the pub in a flurry of activity. Customers stood to congratulate him on his recent interview on Kerry Radio. The barkeeper gestured toward us. John's cheeks were chapped by the wind. He wore a navy wool coat but no hat. His white hair was windblown. Patting it down, he talked to the barkeeper before turning in our direction.

John approached us with outstretched arms. Choosing a seat across from us, he asked how he could be of help. I told him I was related to the Murphy family in Portmagee and that my grandmother was born on Ballyhearney. He remembered the old stone cottage with the thatched roof where Bridget was born. In fact, his father built the newer two-story stone house in 1926 that currently stands on the old site.

He told us about life on Valentia at the time when he and John "Cap" were children in the 1930s. He laughed while recalling how the parish priest refused to attend wakes, since the dancing and partying went on long into the night, with drinking lasting for days after; clay pipes were puffed by everyone attending the wake to signify a temporary truce among the feuding families.

John eagerly entertained us with stories from his childhood. He was familiar with every family on the island and knew about their grandparents' lives during the famine, after the famine, and the years when Ireland seemed forgotten by the rest of the world. John left Valentia to live in London but soon returned to run the family pub.

He pointed to me and asked if I would be ready to marry in the morning. I laughed. He assured us that the young women at that time had no choice in the matter.

On the morning of a wedding, the father of the bride could, and often did, switch daughters if he felt the less attractive one should marry first. What a surprise for the groom, you would think. "Not so," said John. Matches were made for the women of Valentia as late as the 1920s. A man would either buy a donkey or find a woman to marry; they were of the same value to him. But the woman probably worked harder than the donkey. Those were hard times for women as they shouldered not only the responsibility for raising the children, but also helped with the outside chores as well.

John remembered oil lamps and hot water bottles. The doctor, who made house visits, was paid with food produced on the farm. When John ran a small grocery store, he stocked his shelves with loaves of store-baked bread, and any woman who bought that bread was considered lazy and a failure in the eyes of her neighbors. He told about the time a customer owed him a halfpenny. John wasn't worried about the money and told the woman not to give it a thought. During dinner that same evening, John heard someone shuffling around in his store. When he went from his kitchen to the store counter, he spotted the halfpenny she had left. He knew she didn't have a halfpenny and wondered where she had found one for him.

John's ability to tell these stories with humor and perfect delivery kept our attention long into the afternoon. A master at keeping an audience in suspense, he paused at various points in his stories to ask how we thought it would end. We were like obedient school children jumping out of our seats to answer. He, in turn, would grin mischievously and assure us that we were correct.

Sharon Shea Bossard

He recalled his first day of school and the dances on Valentia. As a young man, he'd hurry home from the Ballyhearney School to help set up the dance floor inside the pub. Dancing was a popular pastime, but there were no dance halls. Stages erected for revelers were crowded with people dancing the Irish reel or jig. Before sunrise on the first of May, the islanders would bring a flowering branch of furze into the house or attach it to the outside of the door in celebration of the spring dance. Bonefires (yes, bonefires) crackled amidst the merriment of those dancing. John enlightened us to the fact that the correct term was bonefire because tradition holds there should always be a bone in the fire.

He thought back to the difficult times during World War II, when food and fuel was rationed and sadness touched all of the people's lives on Valentia. He told us the tractor was introduced to rural Ireland in the 1950s, but it wasn't until the 1970s that indoor plumbing with toilets as well as hot and cold running water was brought into the cottages. John remembered his hostel as having the very first indoor bathroom on rural Valentia.

A common island superstition was that it was unlucky to meet a red-haired woman when going fishing, but a black haired one was lucky. A filled pipe would be left out at night for the little fairies or leprechauns so they wouldn't steal the calf. John remembered when a neighbor refused to plow the field behind his cottage because he was sure the fairies lived there. It was luckier to borrow eggs than to sell those from one's own hen. He went on to tell us that if a crow flew west, it meant that a friend or relative in America had just died. And keeping a white cock might result in the death of the head of the house. If the dweller of the cottage carried a dead animal across the stream, it took the bad luck to the other side. It was unlucky to pay out money on Monday, and it was unlucky for a mother to attend the funeral of her first child.

This lovely gentleman with his wonderful stories charmed Phil and me. John wanted us to meet someone that he had known all of his life, and he asked if we would drive him to the townland of Tennes to visit Mary O'Neill.

After a short drive, we pulled in front of a cottage with heavy layers of thatch piled high on top. John told us this was one of two thatched roof dwellings left on the island. Made from bog grass, the roof was held together with ropes and netting to protect it from the winds. It sagged and seemed to weigh down the small place, and I questioned how safe we would be once inside. John laughed. Apparently, he thought I was joking.

He knocked to announce our arrival. The door creaked open letting in a stream of sunlight. Needing a moment for our eyes to adjust to the darkness, we hesitated at the doorway. John called out to Mary. We heard shuffling noises, and the smell of musty, stale air surrounded us. The only light in the cottage came from the few pieces of peat burning in the hearth. John told Mary that he brought visitors from America.

Seated in front of the hearth was an old woman who looked as though time had forgotten. Mary wore an old flowered scarf knotted tightly at her chin. A black tattered wool shawl was pulled across her shoulders. We commented on the beautiful chair in which she sat. She told us her grandfather had made it for her as a wedding gift.

The cottage had two rooms. The floors were stone and the walls were sadly in need of repair. We observed the tiny windows crusted with dirt and the ragged old curtains that hung from a wire attached to the stone by a nail. A worn wooden table with four chairs was pushed into a corner. A small refrigerator hummed loudly, and a bare bulb flickered over the worn, chipped sink. A blackened aluminum kettle, dented and pocked, rested on a grate in the hearth fireplace. Mary offered us tea.

Gnats buzzed overhead while Mary poured from the kettle. Her wrinkled man-sized hands positioned the kettle over delicate china cups. These hands displayed fingers distorted from arthritis, her knuckles gnarled by years of hard work. The corners of Mary's mouth spread into a toothless grin when she was complimented on the lovely tea service. We noticed strands of her brown hair streaked with gray that carelessly trailed out from under her scarf. Mary's life mirrored the life lived by my grandmother one hundred and twenty-four years ago.

Mary told us about her father's landlord, the Knight of Kerry, who evicted families from their dwellings in the late 1800s; evictions of the Irish were common. For over two hundred years the Knights of Kerry controlled large areas of land on Valentia. Anglo-Irish Protestants, the Fitzgerald family titled themselves the Knights of Kerry and enjoyed their luxurious life on the island.

I told Mary something we had learned from documents at the heritage center. In 1891, five cows belonging to my grandmother's brother were taken from him when he couldn't pay the thirteen pounds owed in back rent. Mary wasn't surprised to hear this, for that's how life was under English rule.

Years of hard work and deprivation had taken their toll. Mary was six years old when her mother died. She accepted the responsibility of caring for both her older brother and her father. She learned to cook and to work in the fields. Memories of her life on Valentia continue to haunt her as one of her babies died at birth, ending any hopes of happiness.

John told us when Mary was young she possessed wisdom beyond her years, and he boasted of her intellect. John and Mary were companions at the Ballyhearney School in 1934, the very same school my grandmother attended in the late 1870s. John held Mary's hand and told her about our search for my family. She was happy I had located the Murphy family from Portmagee.

The fumes of the peat made our eyes water, but Mary and John didn't seem to notice. John told us Mary looked tired, and we took that as our cue to leave. When we opened the door, a thin ray of sunlight settled on Mary, and a soft breeze rustled the dusty old curtains.

As we drove away, I turned to catch one last look. I wanted to remember the incredible experience of being with Mary in the old thatched cottage. While John and Phil chatted easily in the front seat, I sat reviewing every second of being with her. She is part of a dying breed of the old world, and I wanted to soak in that essence.

When we drove up to the pub, we noticed the place was crowded with customers; it was time to say good-bye to John. We promised to keep in touch and to visit him on our next trip to the island of Valentia. It wasn't easy to leave, for our days were filled with many incredible discoveries. But it was time to go home to tell my family about their cousins in Ireland and to write this story for my grandparents Michael and Bridget.

Our daughter Jennifer in Killarney, Ireland 2003

Sugrena Famine Cemetery in Cahersiveen, County Kerry

Patrick O'Leary showing us the old church in the cemetery where Cornelius and Ellen Murphy are buried

Cottage of the Murphy brothers in Ballinskelligs, County Kerry

Mary O'Neill in front of her cottage on Valentia Island   2004

Hannah Keating with John and Kitty's first grandchild, Damien O'Connell   1980

*Kitty and John Murphy at their cottage in Portmagee, County Kerry,
Ireland 2004*

Kitty Murphy pouring tea in her dining room 2004

Hannah Keating's cottage on Valentia Island   2004

Path to the townland of Ballyhearney—same path Bridget walked when she left in 1880

Townland of Carhan Lower in Cahersiveen—birthplace of my grandfather   2004

Meeting Kathleen Corless in Kylemore Graveyard   2004

"The Crossroads" where Michael and Bridget danced in the 1870s 2004

Peat Field in Cahersiveen, County Kerry, Ireland   2004

CHAPTER 7

Boyle, County
Roscommon, Ireland

I t was November 2003. We planned to travel to the town where my mother's parents were born: Boyle, County Roscommon, Ireland. In preparation for this trip, we collected birth certificates from Ireland, Naturalization Records from Chicago, Irish Census as well as Chicago Census reports, Irish land valuations, and family stories. The time we spent at the Family History Center in Salt Lake City proved valuable, and researching archival records in Dublin provided us with the additional information needed to help establish facts concerning the lives of my grandparents Michael Healy, and Sarah Beirne who emigrated to America in 1903.

Michael and Sarah had been childhood sweethearts in Ireland. Sarah was born August 4, 1881, in the townland of Ardmoyle. Michael was born June 10, 1879, in the neighboring townland of Carrowkeel. My grandparents lived less than a mile apart.

I remember these grandparents. Michael died in 1950 when I was five. I recall the priest who visited our home to administer the last rites. Grandpa was a good, loving man. He died with only his daughter Helen by his side because his wife, Sarah, didn't seem to care much about him. She died in 1966 and was very different from my grandfather; she never displayed warmth or affection. Because I'd never heard any stories about their lives in Ireland, I'd always wondered about the circumstances that molded them into the grandparents I remember.

The thrill of returning to Ireland overwhelmed me. We left Chicago, bound for Shannon, on a late evening flight. Phil and I settled into our narrow, uncomfortable seats and somehow managed to sleep. We woke when the pilot announced our arrival. I noticed the skies were dark and rain clouds were gathering overhead.

After exiting the airplane, Phil and I separated. I joined the line indicating Resident/EU Citizen, while Phil waited to be processed through Immigration. One of the many rewards for researching my Irish lineage was an Irish passport. Holding up the red-colored passport bearing the imprint of an Irish harp, I continued through the busy arrival area to meet Phil. We hopped on the shuttle for the short ride to the rental car lot. We received a stick shift Ford Fiesta, which was good news. It would provide economy along with ease of maneuverability on the narrow roads.

The skies opened in a torrential downpour. We drove out of the airport, while searching for the heat and defroster controls. Traffic was light; this pleased us, for it was difficult enough to drive on the left side of the road without having to worry about congestion. A small decal attached to the passenger side window instructed us to look right and stay left, so I repeated that instruction to

Phil at each intersection. Thank goodness for the round-about. It gave us time to circle while we confirmed our direction. Every road sign was printed in Gaelic as well as in English, so we had to be sure to look for a word that matched the name of a town on our map.

Sheets of rain flooded our windshield. The roads were so narrow that it was difficult to drive without encroaching onto the adjoining lane. We had a couple of close calls, where our car scraped along the hedgerows and I wondered how long it would be before we lost a hubcap or a side view mirror.

The drenching rain and the thick hedgerows obstructed our view. Truck traffic increased as we headed for the town of Tuam; it was time to stop, stretch, and check our route. We thought we might have missed a sign and needed to make sure we were still headed in the right direction. Squinting through the heavy rain, we spied a brightly lit petrol station. Phil remembered to look left while turning right and managed to guide us into the parking area. Sorry to leave the warmth of the car, we decided to run through the puddles to reach shelter inside the station.

A flurry of activity greeted us. Students were clustered at the candy counter, while long lines of patrons snaked down the aisle along the sandwich island. A young woman behind the counter smiled, and I interpreted that as an invitation to ask directions. She glanced at our map, pushed it aside, and wrote the directions to Boyle on a register receipt. Towns with the names of Dunmore, Williamstown, Castlerea, Frenchpark, and Boyle rolled off her pen. The route she suggested would save us an hour of driving time.

While we waited for the heavy rain to slow to a drizzle, we shopped for snacks. Items were pricey, since the exchange rate was not in our favor. At the cash register, we rolled off a Twenty Eurodollar from our small bundle of money. The change was returned in coin, giving us the impression that we had spent a small fortune on chips and soda.

The rain showed no sign of let-up, so we hurried out the door. We stowed our snacks, spread our wet map on the backseat, and headed to Dunmore. While I searched the road signs for the English translations of the Gaelic, the rain continued its unrelenting assault on two weary tourists. Oversized lorries splashed muddy water onto our windshield, and I worried we'd miss the towns of Williamstown and Castlerea.

Driving the country roads in Ireland is much like wandering through a maze. The narrow roads meander through the countryside, while grazing sheep wander onto the roadways and cling to the shoulders, noses buried in the grass and weeds, oblivious to tourists in their midst. I enjoyed the scenery while Phil worked to stay focused on the road. He was the Marco Polo on this trip; his keen sense of direction along with his bravery assured our safety.

I alerted Phil to the possibility that we might have missed a road marker. We weren't able to read the small sign at the bottom of the post, so we circled the roundabout a few times until we located our destination—Boyle! We continued our drive through Frenchpark, knowing that soon we would be in the village of my grandparents.

After years of researching townlands, villages, and

parishes, I was finally able to match those names to this place in Ireland. Signs identified Balinameen, Breedogue, and the old Kingsland School. Tiny, old cottages were scattered along the flat narrow road. We passed St. Bridget's Church—my grandparents' church. With nowhere to make the turnaround safely, we decided to continue to Boyle in order to secure a room for the night. Tomorrow, we would return.

We continued down the road. Through the mist, I spotted an untended graveyard and wondered if my great-grandparents were buried there. From our vantage point, the tombstones appeared to float through the fog. Surrounded by a broken-down fence, the old gravestones were crowded together and heaved from the earth in disarray. We had so much to find on this trip.

I recalled reading about the fairs and markets known as the "farmers stock exchange" that were held in Boyle, dating back to the sixth century. Cattle were gathered from the fields in the dark of night by the farmers, who walked alongside them along the road with the aid of a lantern. For those who were ten miles away, the journey began as early as four o'clock in the morning. Farmers arrived in Boyle by seven o'clock, the exact hour the bidding began. When a cow was purchased, a spit on the hand accompanied by a hand slap would seal the deal. This road to Boyle was the same one that led to the fairs and markets in years past. My grandparents and their ancestors had participated in that walk to the fair.

My fingers searched for the edge of the seat, and I wrapped them tightly around the cool steel frame. It helped to keep me focused, for I was dizzy with anticipation of our arrival. I also couldn't wait for tomorrow to walk along the same road that took my grandparents into Boyle over one hundred years ago.

We rounded a corner and entered the village of Boyle, pausing at the top of a hill to view rooftops in colors of reds, yellows, and blues. The fog hadn't yet seeped into the town. Phil pulled the car to the side of the road so we could enjoy the amazing scenery. Soft green meadows dotted with purple heather wound their way to the cottages nestled on the hillsides. The charming village of Boyle rests comfortably amidst the most beautiful landscape imaginable.

With the town square to our right and a small grocery to our left, we began our descent into Boyle. Late afternoon shoppers hurried for shelter from the rain. Red hair and flashing blue eyes, partially hidden under woolen caps, gave me pause to contemplate my place among these Irish. I already felt camaraderie with these townspeople, and I wondered just how much I would learn from this visit.

From pictures of Boyle dating back to the late 1800s, it appeared that the town had remained largely unchanged. The curbs gave way to wide streets, and the bridge crossing the Boyle River looked just the same as it did in 1903—the year my grandparents left for America. The old buildings welcomed visitors with their colorful doors and window boxes filled with late fall flowers.

It was easy to imagine the town of Boyle one hundred years ago, my grandparents walking these streets and crossing the old bridge. Michael, along with his two brothers and his sister, came into town to sell their goods. Barefoot and dressed in tattered clothing, they looked no different from the rest of the farm children. Shoes were a luxury, and they were worn only for church or when the weather turned unusually cold.

The extraordinary circumstances that ravaged Boyle during the Famine of 1846 had been wiped away by time. The recent strong economy provides the residents with modern conveniences as well as a range of opportunities. Looking over the landscape with its rolling hills and scenic beauty, it defied all sensible thinking to imagine that one morning a hundred and fifty years ago the people of Ireland woke up to the smell of rotting potatoes. They had labored in fields harvesting oats, barley, and wheat in abundance. Boats laden with all those good nutritious grains grown on Irish soil were sent to England. The oats, barley, and wheat were not for the Irish; their allotment was the rotted potato.

Michael and Sarah dreamed about their new lives in America. The ramblers who visited their cottages told them stories of how, in America, the streets were paved in gold. They filled their heads with visions of fortune and promises of happiness, for how could you not be happy while enjoying all the comforts of the rich? I imagined they listened with an eager curiosity.

My grandparents were children of famine survivors. They lived in poverty on family farms that were owned by the English landlord. Any money the family managed to save went to pay the rent. The only way they could emigrate to America was if a family member already in America sent money for their passage. According to ship records, John Healy sponsored Michael, and Patrick Beirne sponsored Sarah. I never knew that my grandparents had brothers, because they never spoke a word about them to any of us. There was so much we didn't know, and I hoped this trip would satisfy my need to learn whatever I could about this family.

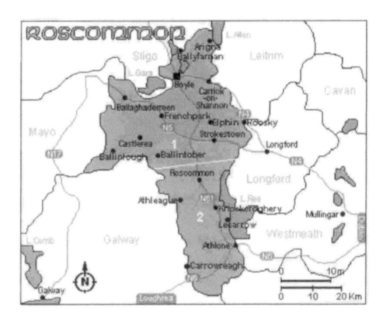

CHAPTER 8

Searching for the Healy Family

We located a charming bed and breakfast outside of town. It was the perfect place to stay for the three nights we planned to spend in Boyle. Already past the point of requiring sleep, we agreed to spend what little time there was left of the afternoon to explore the town. We freshened up and headed out the door.

A road sign indicating tourist information ahead led us to the King House. It had been abandoned in the eighteenth century and served as a military barracks for the officially titled British Army Regiment in my grandfather's time. The King House wasn't a dwelling but rather a symbol of the power and status of the landlord during and after the famine. An information office was located at this site, and we thought it would be a good place to stop and ask directions.

We found a parking space one block away, grabbed our umbrellas, and ran to the entrance. It was closed, but we noticed a small gift shop next door and thought maybe someone in there could help us. We were at a loss as to how to begin our search; besides, we needed to get out of the rain.

Bells chimed, alerting the clerk to our arrival. The aroma of incense, and the sounds of soft music encircled us. That surprised us because, from the outside, the shop looked unkempt. We were pleased to see a tidy little souvenir shop. The entire back wall held books and maps, and I headed there in search of a local Ordinance Survey but found nothing. I asked the shopkeeper where the townlands of Carrowkeel and Ardmoyle might be located. She had no idea but suggested we visit Kevin O'Sullivan, who worked in a shoe store/mortuary in the town of Sligo—a shoe store and a mortuary? Now that sounded interesting! The shopkeeper suggested we take the local bus and then we wouldn't have to move our car because parking was a problem.

We ran to our car just as the skies opened again. We thought for a moment that we could wait for the bus but decided not to risk getting soaked. Besides, the thought of having to purchase another pair of shoes—from an undertaker—didn't appeal to either of us.

Dusk blanketed the town; traffic was heavy. The windshield wipers were losing their battle to the endless downpour. Both of us spotted the shop at the same time and laughed when we read the awning—a shoe shop and mortician. A creepy feeling came over me, and I hoped not to spend too much time in that place.

We parked across the street and hurried inside, stomping our soggy shoes on the mat and storing our umbrellas by the door. An older, full-faced woman with a thick brogue greeted us. We asked if Kevin O'Sullivan was available; she went to find him. Meanwhile, we looked around the store wondering which shoes were for the deceased. The shoes and boots were pricey, leaving me to conclude that the residents of this area must be doing pretty well financially.

Kevin appeared from the back room, wiping his hands on a wrinkled towel. I didn't want to imagine what he was doing back there. I quickly introduced us, and when Mr. O'Sullivan extended his hand in a warm greeting, I cautiously accepted.

I told him about our search for the Healy family. He looked surprised and then invited us to have a seat. Kevin told us that he had known Johnny Healy McCarthy from Carrowkeel. He told us that Johnny had lived with his uncle Peter Healy. Peter Healy! That was one of the names on the 1901 Irish Census. I knew that Peter was my grandfather's brother, but who was Johnny? Not wanting to interrupt, I listened while Kevin explained that both Peter and Johnny had remained bachelors. He told us that there were hurtful feelings between the families of the Healys and McCarthys. I was confused about the McCarthy name.

I knew from information on the 1901 Irish Census that Peter had stayed in Ireland to care for their elderly father. Peter's brother Michael and their sister Maggie had left Ireland in 1903. Since there was only one sister, and she emigrated with my grandfather, then who was Johnny's mother? Kevin told us that Johnny was Maggie's son. So, Maggie had returned to Ireland. What an unexpected turn of events! I always thought the Irish who left, never returned.

I asked Kevin about Maggie. He didn't remember her because Maggie died in 1932 at the age of fifty-four. Kevin began work at the mortuary in 1945. I knew from the Passenger Manifest that Michael and Maggie traveled to Bridgeport, Connecticut to meet up with their brother John. And now I learned that Maggie returned to Ireland. She probably came back to Carrowkeel to help care for her brother Peter and their elderly father, or perhaps she returned to a man she loved. And maybe that man was a McCarthy.

Unfortunately, the McCarthy man didn't love Maggie as much as she loved him because he didn't marry her and give his baby a proper name. That was scandalous behavior in 1908—the year Johnny was born.

It occurred to me that Maggie's father might have been happy to send his only daughter to America to get her away from the McCarthy man. For whatever reason, Maggie returned and got pregnant. She was twenty-eight years old, not a love struck teenager by any means; I wondered what the real story was.

I had read that the Catholic Church scorned unwed mothers and branded them as sinners. In those days, the girls were locked away in convents and their babies given away to English families. Maggie was spared the humiliation of the convent laundry because of her father's devotion to her. Johnny's father emigrated to America before Johnny was born. Talk in the town was that he left behind the son who would live his entire life on Carrowkeel as an outcast because he was born out of wedlock.

Customers were crowding into the shoe store, distracting Kevin. I knew he was busy, but I was riveted to my chair. We never expected to find out so much about the Healy family. I asked Kevin if there was anything else he could remember. He told us we would learn more by talking to the neighbors. Neighbors! Somehow, I never expected to be talking to anyone who lived in the Healy neighborhood. Kevin cautioned us to approach the neighbors carefully, as our visit might be viewed suspiciously.

Kevin told us it was too bad we hadn't come sooner because Peter was buried in 1964 and Johnny in 1997. I felt sorrow for all the unhappiness that had surrounded the Healy family.

I mentioned my grandmother's family and asked if he knew of them. Kevin recalled a Beirne family from the townland of Ardmoyle, but he didn't think that any of those family members had left Ireland. Then he pulled out a piece of notepaper and drew a map to Carrowkeel. I asked him to also show us where the cemetery was. Kevin said we had passed it on our way into town. So, the graveyard we saw on our drive into Boyle is the final resting place of my grandfather's family, and because the townlands of Carrowkeel and Ardmoyle bordered each other, I wondered if my grandmother's parents were buried there as well.

A sense of loss washed over me, and I wondered about my second cousin Johnny, who lived alone on Carrowkeel. Why didn't our family know about him? It was difficult for me to imagine why they hadn't kept in touch with one another. I understood more clearly the regrettable circumstances that influenced my grandparents' lives in America. They were never happy, and maybe now I could find out why.

Kevin wrote down the name and address of an old man who might be able to answer our questions, Frank McCarthy, and directed us to take the road to Frenchpark and then to watch for the fourth house past the first pub on the right. Kevin went on to tell us that Frank was eighty-five years old and very crabby, and cautioned us to be sure the window shades were pulled up before we knocked on his door. If they weren't, we should return later in the day.

Kevin said the Healy cottage was still there; in fact, he had driven by it a few months ago and noticed a new roof. The cottage stood vacant since Johnny's death. Just then, the phone rang and Kevin needed to answer it. It was time for us to leave. Thanking him for his help, we said good-bye and told him we would return to let him know what we found.

Phil and I walked to the nearest pub. Besides being hungry, we needed to digest all we'd learned from Kevin. When we opened the narrow doors, the sweet smell of the peat fire drew us in. The only sounds were those of the bar patrons, and we wondered if the place served food. That question was answered soon enough, for the barkeeper invited us in to sit close to the fire and then asked if we were hungry.

We pulled our chairs next to the hearth to warm ourselves. The embers from the fire glowed red hot, and I slipped off my shoes and warmed my feet. We didn't realize how cold and wet we were until we began to peel away the layers of damp clothing.

The menu wasn't elaborate, and that pleased us. A simple meal of soup and sandwich was just what we needed before turning in for the night. Phil and I talked about our recent discovery and couldn't believe our good fortune in finding out that the Healy cottage remained intact. As tired as we were, we had just enough energy left to plan our next day's activity, which included finding the person who could open the cottage to us. As Kevin suggested, we would talk to the neighbors.

I hoped the Beirne cottage would be easy to find. It didn't surprise me that Kevin had no recollection of any Beirne family who emigrated, because my family left in 1903. According to the Passenger Manifest, all the Beirne children emigrated to America after their parents had died.

We lingered at the pub just long enough to finish a pot of tea. The warm beverage was delicious; it provided the soothing calm to our busy day. We reached for our coats, which were now dry and toasty warm and reluctantly left the shelter of the pub for the rain-filled streets of Sligo. We ran to the car, dodging huge raindrops and noticed it was now sleeting. We hoped for a much better day tomorrow, for we had lots of work ahead of us.

CHAPTER 9

Into the Country

Long before the rooster crowed, I woke. I rested in bed, thinking about the Healy family, trying to imagine how difficult their lives must have been. They certainly suffered their share of sadness in Ireland. If my grandfather had known about their problems, would he have returned? Maggie did. After braving the difficult sea voyage to finally arrive at Ellis Island, Maggie left America to go back to the drafty old thatched cottage where her father and brother still lived. Her loyalty to family in Ireland proved stronger than her ties to America. Or, could it have been her love for the McCarthy man?

Lingering over breakfast, Phil and I discussed our concern about visiting Frank McCarthy. Why would Kevin direct us to a McCarthy, knowing that the families didn't get along? We guessed we would find out soon enough. I grabbed my briefcase and placed Kevin's map to Carrowkeel in my pocket. Gathering our courage, we headed for the McCarthy cottage.

On the road to Frenchpark, the Killarght Graveyard came into view, an eerie looking place in the early morn-

ing with the dew rising to a frosty mist. The few gravestones that I saw through the fog were crooked and moss
covered, and I wondered how many generations of my
ancestors were there.

I thought of my great-grandparents buried in that dilapidated old cemetery and remembered what Patrick
O'Leary from Ballinskelligs had told us about the Irish
burial traditions. Up to nine generations of the same family shared one grave. The body and the wooden coffin usually decomposed after fifteen years, mixing their dust with
the dust of their ancestors—a stark contrast to my grandparents' graves in America, which were carpeted in lush
green grass and marked with shiny marble headstones,
their remains, each encased in bronze-lined waterproof
cement boxes. Kevin O'Sullivan told us how he dreaded
receiving the deceased from America because the coffins
were large and the hinged lids were difficult to work with.
He preferred the narrow wooden boxes with removable
tops. Those deteriorated, whereas, the elaborate metal
coffins from America didn't.

My great-grandparents survived the potato famine.
Other famines followed as others had gone before, but it
was the Great Hunger of 1845 that made the Irish household suffer the most.

I recalled my Irish history. The Penal Laws of 1695
made the Irish slaves. Catholics were prohibited from buying land, bringing up their children in the Catholic faith,
or entering law enforcement. By 1778, Irish Catholics
owned only 5% of Irish land. Catholic priests who didn't
conform to the laws were frequently branded on the face
or castrated. All Irish culture, music, and education were

banned. My ancestors suffered undue hardships while living under British rule. In 1801, The Act of Union was put into force, which brought Ireland completely under British subjugation.

My great-grandfathers rented their ancestral land from the English to grow potatoes, and they worked a given number of days for the landlord as part payment of the rent. If they had a pig, a cow, or some chickens, they would share the hearth at night to prevent someone from stealing them. A dung heap, located next to the entrance of the cottage, was a symbol of wealth, not poverty. This abundance of manure provided the fertilizer that nourished the land and allowed for a healthy crop of potato.

My Irish ancestors never handled money; in fact, they wouldn't be able to recognize its worth because they never used it for legal tender. It was considered a crime in some townlands to carry any currency. The Irish lived entirely under the rule of their English landlords, and, unfortunately, they relied solely on the potato for their existence.

According to records contained in the Tithe Applotment Books, my great-grandfather William Healy was born in a hut on Carrowkeel in the year 1806. The walls of the hut were formed by the backs of fences, the floors sunk into the ditches, the height scarcely enough for a man to stand upright. Poles not thicker than a broomstick for supports and a few pieces of grass sod afforded the only roof covering.

In 1821, the year William Healy turned fifteen, Catholics began to make demands for religious liberty. His landlord, Lord Lorton, declared that Catholics weren't welcome at the meetings to discuss repeal of the Penal Laws.

All the tenant farmers in Boyle feared Lord Lorton because he severely punished those Catholics caught in secret planning meetings to overthrow the Protestant religion.

In 1847, when William was forty-one, famine hit the village of Boyle. Starving, ragged, disease-ridden peasants roamed the countryside in search of food and shelter. The poor farmers who couldn't pay their rent were evicted from their cottages. Many of the Irish were forced to burn the corpses and homes of their neighbors so they wouldn't catch famine fever or typhus. My great-grandfather's family lived at a time when men, women, and children died miserably in ditches, in fields, and on roadsides. He was among those fortunate enough to survive those horrible times.

Lord Lorton passed ownership of the Healy land to Edward King-Harmon in 1872. My great-grandfather's dream to one day own the land of his ancestors was finally realized when he purchased his land in 1908; he was 102 years old. I often think that the burning desire to own his land was what kept him alive for so long.

The countryside hadn't changed much since the time of my great-grandfather; the ancient stone cottages could be seen from the road. Farmers still use the old dirt paths traveled on hundreds of years ago.

We spotted the pub on the left and knew that Frank McCarthy's cottage was close. The house looked like a haunted mansion; it was over-run with weeds and ugly vines. Thorn bushes grew up along the sides, covering the upstairs windows. We hesitated at the entrance because the shades were pulled down. That was our cue to drive on, as Kevin had warned us, and we were relieved to do so.

Checking the map, we proceeded down the road to Carrowkeel. Last night the directions seemed clear. This morning they were difficult to follow; none of the roads were marked with signs.

A mile down the road, we found Flanagan's Pub. It used to be the old Kingsland Pub next door to the Kingsland School where my grandparents were students in 1890. I told Phil that later we should visit the old pub and talk with some of the neighbors who might possibly remember the Healys or Beirnes. For now, we were focused on finding their cottages.

We were amazed at how narrow the pavement was. It wouldn't be possible to drive without leaving the road if someone approached from the opposite direction. We saw neither cottages nor signs of life in the area.

Further down the road, we spotted a car parked off to the side and saw an old man walking with a cane; he was headed into the pasture. Phil parked behind the old man's car, and I slid out of my seat and hurried to catch up with him. When I called out, he turned to walk toward me. I could see he was nicely dressed. Under his overcoat he wore a suit, a white shirt, and a tie. His dress pants were tucked into high rubber boots. He wore the same kind of cap that my grandfather had worn years ago. As he approached me, I could see that his shirt collar was torn at the crease; his clumsily knotted tie hung crookedly under the collar points. He was clean-shaven and walked very erect; I guessed his age to be about eighty.

I introduced myself and told him we were looking for the Healy cottage on Carrowkeel. He stepped back in surprise when he heard I was the grandniece of Peter Healy and the second cousin to Johnny. I explained that my grandfather was Peter's brother and showed him a copy of the 1901 Irish Census. I could tell by the look on his face that he had never seen a census report. When he pulled out his glasses from the pocket of his overcoat, I noticed they needed a good cleaning. He looked at his boots and poked his cane into the mud before telling us that Peter and Johnny were good men. I asked if he could help us locate their cottage. Reaching for the census paper, he agreed to show us the way.

He introduced himself as Liam McCarthy. When I mentioned we were going to visit a Frank McCarthy to ask about the Healy family, he told us not to bother as we would be wasting our time. Frank is his brother. I asked if they were any relation to Johnny Healy McCarthy. Liam didn't respond to my question. Instead, he pointed to the camera on the back seat of our car. Then he asked Phil to take a picture of him with me. I wasn't prepared for what happened next.

Liam asked me for a kiss. Then he told Phil to take a picture of us, kissing. Feeling sorry for this old man, I gave him a peck on the cheek, but he wasn't satisfied with that and he pushed his face into mine and planted a big wet kiss on my mouth. Then he slapped my backside. What was going on? I reminded him that he needed to show us how to get to Carrowkeel. I looked over at Phil and could see that he was just as surprised as I was by what had just occurred. As humorous as the situation seemed, I had mixed feelings. There was a part of me that wanted to slug him and another part of me that felt sorry for him. It was obvious that Liam was quite pleased with his morning's activity because he asked if we would send him some of the pictures. While he wrote down his address, I asked again if he was related to Johnny. Thinking he might be deaf, I repeated the question. It became apparent that he had no intention of responding.

He pointed directly across his pasture and told us that the Healy cottage was on the other side. His said to follow the road to the bend, and when we came to a wider road, turn right. There we would find the cottage. I asked Liam how many roads would we pass before turning right onto Carrowkeel? He couldn't tell us that because he only knew that it was directly across the pasture. I asked how old he was; he said he was ninety-two. That old man was in pretty good shape for his age! He waved good-bye and then headed back into the field in search of his bull. We wondered about that interesting encounter and hoped he would be safe. Now our task was to find the boundary of Liam's pasture.

Further down the road, we approached a herd of cows taking their time crossing the road. We crept behind them, keeping a safe distance so as not to frighten them. Then a small blue car turned onto our road. It stopped, and the driver waved us on. He joined our "cow parade." We were hardly moving and getting antsy. Thinking that the cows were walking the seven miles into Boyle, we thought it best to find another route as we didn't want to drive the next half hour in back of the herd.

I stepped out of our car to ask the driver behind us if he could suggest an alternate route. A large, muscular man squeezed behind the wheel of a compact car greeted me warmly. His smile was wide; his eyes reflected the gray-blue of the morning sky. He was handsome, and I could see that he was also a farmer. The front of his heavy wool coat bunched into the steering wheel; a labor-calloused hand gripped the bowl of an old pipe. His face showed the features of a man who made his living toiling in the fields. I bid him good morning and inquired as to the quickest route to the other side of the pasture. He assured me that our wait wouldn't be too long, and he asked that we stay a little farther back from the herd. I imagined this would make interesting pub conversation—Americans looking for the fastest route! It was a pretty good bet that tourists didn't travel these backcountry roads very often. I thanked him for his help, returned to our car, and told Phil how friendly and helpful he was. Within a few minutes the cows spilled into their pasture, and we were on our way to Carrowkeel. Or at least, we hoped we were.

We rounded the bend and continued following the pasture boundary. Confused as to what was a road and what was a cow path, we agreed to continue going straight until we came to a road that seemed to be well traveled; we hoped that Carrowkeel was on a paved road.

Phil stopped in front of an old stone building. He was sure he found my grandfather's place; however, I didn't think so because what he found looked like an old neglected barn. The census described the Healy cottage as having three windows and a door on the front. No, that wasn't it. I asked Phil to drive up the road, for maybe we could find someone to help us.

We stopped to ask directions from five different farmers. Each of them was either on his tractor or getting ready to climb onto one. They all knew the Healys and were pleased to meet us. When I mentioned we were from

Chicago, one of the farmers asked if that was at the far end of America. He had heard of California and was sure most Americans lived there. We spoke of Peter's brothers John and Michael, who emigrated to America. They had never heard about Peter's brothers.

My heart ached for Peter. I understood that the Irish wake meant that family members who left were as good as dead, yet, they could have stayed in touch—why didn't they? Surely his brothers would have contacted him, if not to let him know they were safe, at least to share stories about their families. There was so much to learn about the Healys and the Beirnes. It was already way past noon and we had yet to find Carrowkeel.

One of the farmers climbed off his tractor and walked with us to the other side of the road. He pointed at a rooftop peeking up from the valley. At last! We had found the Healy cottage. He told us that Johnny had willed the cottage to a neighbor, Tom Cleary. Then he pointed to where Tom lived, just up the road.

Phil knew the road that would take us there. We traveled down an extremely narrow passage and passed a stone cottage. Phil stepped on the brakes, and we both turned to look back. There was a nervous feeling in the pit of my stomach, and I didn't know whether or not I would be able to get out of the car. My dream of finding something—anything—belonging to a grandparent had materialized.

We looked at the abandoned cottage where my grandfather Michael was born in 1879. This was also the home of my great-grandfather's first wife and family in the 1820s. On August 15, 1867, at the age of sixty-one, my great-grandfather married his second wife Ellen, a cousin. Ellen was only twenty-three and young enough to bear him four more children. She died from a stomachache in this cottage on May 27, 1896, at the age of fifty-two. William died on February 7, 1910, of old age—104. William and Ellen had raised their four children: Maggie, John, Michael, and Peter in this cottage on Carrowkeel.

There was so much family history attached to the old cottage. I imagined my young grandfather with suitcase in hand leaving for America at the age of twenty-two; Maggie was twenty-five. They left the security of their home to venture into the unknown—America held their dreams.

The farm was small by today's standards—only twenty acres. The pastures were overgrown with tall field grasses mixed with purple forget-me-nots. Standing in front of the cottage, I closed my eyes to imagine the smell of peat burning on the hearth, the sound of spades digging vegetables from the earth, and leaves rustling in the wind. A gust of cold air swirled around me; the skies darkened. Thunder rumbled in the distance. I touched the door, the windows, and the old stone walls. I leaned against the building to rest my cheek on the cold stone.

Cupping my hands for a better view, I peered into the windows. Ragged lace curtains, thick with dust, partially covered the grimy windowpanes. The cottage was dark, making it difficult to see anything inside. I spotted a small china dog that had been placed on the windowsill and wondered if Johnny had put it there, or maybe Peter. The anticipation of finding something in the old cottage that had belonged to my family encouraged me. I turned to look for Phil. We had to find Tom Cleary and ask if he would let us inside.

CHAPTER 10

Carrowkeel and Ardmoyle

A flash of lightning ripped through the sky followed by a loud clap of thunder; wind gusts slammed against the metal gate, breaking the eerie silence. Phil came running from the back of the cottage as I sprinted toward the road. Scrambling into the car, Phil started the engine while he searched for the heat and defroster knobs. The skies opened and the rain poured down.

My grandfather's sad, unkempt cottage looked dreary through the steady downpour. The transoms above the windows had been left open and the rain soaked the old ragged curtains that drooped from a makeshift rod. For hundreds of years this cottage had sheltered the Healy family, but no longer. No one dug turf, planted gardens, herded cattle, or celebrated the harvest. Since Johnny's death, the cottage stood as silent as the grave.

Kevin O'Sullivan had suggested we talk with the neighbors. Through the rain, we spotted two cottages, one down from the Healy place that sat back off the road, partially hidden by the bushes; the other more modern-looking, lay closer to the road. The rain slowed to a drizzle. Phil waited in the car while I ran to the front door of the more modern-looking cottage. Standing under the shelter of an awning, I knocked loudly enough to be heard over the distant rumblings of thunder. A pretty red-haired girl answered the door. She had striking green eyes that sparkled when she smiled. When I inquired about the Healy family, she directed us to Bridie Doyle's cottage next door. Bridie, at the age of ninety-five, lived alone and had known the Healy family all of her life. The young girl offered to ring Bridie up to alert her of our arrival.

Bridie's cottage looked exactly like my grandfather's. Small and unkempt, both showed every bit of their age of over two hundred years. We could see the white stone through the bushy, untended front yard, and I couldn't wait to be invited inside. I wanted to see her place, just in case we failed to find Tom with the key to my grandfather's house.

The front door swung open, and a smiling Bridie welcomed us in from the rain. We dried our shoes on the worn carpet by the door and asked if she would prefer we remove them. She laughed while assuring us that we could leave them on because she had not yet swept. Her floors sparkled. They were covered in modern vinyl linoleum. The busy pattern wound its way into each of the tiny rooms off the hall. Bridie guided us into her kitchen and immediately stacked more peat logs onto the fire. The old peat stove radiated enough heat to warm the tidy two-bedroom cottage.

I noticed two upholstered chairs, a small sink, one radio, and two pictures of the Sacred Heart of Jesus. These cottages were built without parlors or bathrooms. Indoor bathrooms came only fifteen years ago in the neighborhood of Carrowkeel, either small room additions at the rear of the cottage or installed in the corner of a bedroom.

Bridie told us she was born in the bedroom off the kitchen, and that she had given birth to her three children in that same room. And most likely, she would be waked in the cottage. She spoke of one son who took her to the Post on the first Friday of each month to collect her pension check. Although her pension was small, it helped her to buy a few groceries and a pint of good Irish whiskey every now and then.

A rough wooden table located under the kitchen window served as a work surface as well as her dining room, and it allowed Bridie a view of the road while she prepared and ate her meals. It looked as though we had interrupted her soup making; freshly cut carrots and turnips looked ready to be added to the soup pot. An oilcloth runner covered the table that was probably as old as she. Starched lace curtains hung stiffly at the window, keeping out any ray of sunlight that could have brightened the dingy room. One converted gas lamp dangled from the ceiling on a thick black electrical cord. The upholstered chairs had been arranged close to the hearth, and the peat fire was blazing.

Bridie's brogue was musical. She offered us tea, while digging through her metal cabinet for cookies. I told her who we were and why we had come. Hearing the name of Healy brought tears to her eyes. Bridie walked over to the hearth and removed the aluminum teakettle from the grate. While crossing the room to the sink, she spoke with sadness of Peter, Maggie, and Johnny. She fondly remembered

Maggie and recalled how her children loved to visit her because she kept an interesting old clock underneath her bed. It didn't work but the children loved to look at the delicate carving and the Roman numerals. Bridie's youngest son had a crush on Maggie; he would call to her whenever he saw her working in the field. To this day, if she listens carefully, she can still hear her son's voice and Maggie's voice drifting in from the yard as if it were yesterday.

Her husband Mick palled around with Johnny; they worked odd jobs around the neighborhood after Peter Healy died. She told us it was many an evening that Johnny relaxed by their hearth, not so keen on going home to an empty cottage. We asked if he ever had a girlfriend. Bridie told us that there had been couple of girls he liked, but he never went out with them. She lowered her voice while telling us it was the McCarthy family who ruined Johnny's life; they never accepted him as one of their own.

Bridie settled into a hard-backed wooden chair in the corner and told stories about the Healy family. Peter took good care of his sister Maggie and her son Johnny. They were a good family, a happy family, and they survived on very little. After Maggie died in 1932, their world fell apart; they missed her terribly. Never having found women they wanted to marry, they remained bachelors all their lives. Johnny left for England in 1934. He, along with Bridie's brother-in-law, went in search of work to earn enough to pay off their cottages. When the Second World War broke out in Europe, Peter asked Johnny to return to Carrowkeel.

Before Peter died, both he and Johnny worked as carpenters. They built barns, room additions, constructed stone fences, and did all sorts of construction jobs for their neighbors. They earned a few Irish pounds to spend at the Kingsland Pub, and Johnny was able to attend the cinema in Boyle every week to see the latest picture show. They were generous, and their door was always open for the neighbors and any hungry travelers who happened by.

Bridie remembered the day when Peter returned from the town fair with a huge piece of furniture teetering on his donkey cart. The neighbors gathered to watch as he and Johnny barely squeezed the beautifully carved wooden breakfront into their small kitchen.

Wiping away her tears, Bridie noticed that she hadn't put the teakettle on the hearth and asked us if we'd like some whiskey instead. We declined; we didn't wish to interrupt her stories. Pouring herself a wee drink, she went on to tell us about Johnny's dark moods. Ten years before his death, Johnny's behavior became unstable. He loved to hunt the Irish hare, and one day he appeared at her window with the loaded rifle. Johnny looked angry and she was afraid. Bridie's husband took Johnny home and settled him down. She thought his strange behavior had something to do with his frequent nosebleeds because after a nosebleed, he returned to his old self. Ultimately, Johnny suffered from loneliness, and he became suspicious of everyone who knocked on his door.

We asked Bridie about Tom Cleary and why Johnny had willed the cottage to him. She said that Tom helped Johnny when no one else could. Then we asked about the name of McCarthy. Bridie shook her head and told us how the two families disliked one another. If Johnny happened to be talking to a neighbor and a McCarthy man passed, he would greet the neighbor but not Johnny. Johnny lived with this rejection his entire life. He only used the surname McCarthy because he wanted all of Boyle to know that if there was any money to be had, he deserved his share. This thinking went unrewarded. The McCarthy family shunned Johnny every chance they got.

Bridie thought she might have a picture of Johnny somewhere in her attic. She apologized for not serving us tea but thanked us for stopping by to visit. We were grateful for her time and assured her that we would return for the picture the next day.

Before leaving, I had one more question for Bridie. I asked if Peter or Maggie ever talked about their two brothers who left for America. Bridie thought for a moment and shook her head. As long as she had known the Healy family, she heard nothing of any brothers in America. I would have thought at some time the conversation between neighbors would have included their brothers who emigrated. So, it was true what they said about the Irish wakes. Those who emigrated were as good as dead to the family left behind. Then we asked if she could point us to Tom's cottage. Bridie told us to make a right turn once out of her driveway and then go to the main road and after a left turn, we would see it.

Bridie's directions were difficult to follow because there were many smaller side roads off the larger one. However, we did end up in front of a two-story brick cottage on the road that everyone seemed to point to when directing us to Tom's cottage. A rope stretched across the driveway warned us of newly poured concrete. I got out of the car to climb over the front stone fence, lest I leave footprints and maybe my shoes in the new cement. There was no answer to my persistent knocking, so I went around to the back. The curtains were drawn, and I couldn't see any signs of life in the barn, either. When I returned to the car, I suggested to Phil that we come back in the morning. If Tom was a farmer, it was a good bet he was out with the cows.

When the skies cleared, we found ourselves with a couple of hours of daylight left. We thought a visit to the Killarght Graveyard might turn up some clues. Since we had passed the graveyard so many times in our search for the cottage, Phil had no trouble finding the entrance. We pulled in and left our car by the gate. A huge wooden cross was centered in the middle of the rocky, weed-infested cemetery. Some of the gravestones were so old the script had worn away, making it difficult to read the names of the deceased or their dates of death. Many of the old stones had fallen onto the graves of others. We walked along the back, being careful not to get a foot caught in the hidden gullies and weed-covered crevices.

Phil located the Healy tombstone. We read the names Peter Healy, Margaret Healy, and Johnny McCarthy. So, Johnny took that name to his grave. We guessed it was his last-chance gesture to intentionally thumb his nose at that family. This didn't surprise us. From the stories we had heard about Johnny, we pictured him with spirit.

I looked past the tombstones to the pastures where dozens of sheep grazed. The wind blew strong, and the rain-drenched clouds hung thick overhead. It seemed as if Phil and I were the only two people in the world; there was nothing but peaceful pasture all around. The impending storm didn't deter us from remaining at their gravestone, and I hoped they knew we were there. I knelt to touch the grave. I wanted to connect with their spirits and pray for their souls.

We wandered around the area searching for the graves of my grandmother's parents, John Beirne, who died in 1897, and Mary Beirne, in 1896. After stumbling over numerous scattered rocks and getting tangled in prickly weeds, we gave up our search. We had an hour before nightfall and decided to try and locate the townland of Ardmoyle, the birthplace of my grandmother Sarah Beirne.

We drove on the road to Frenchpark and turned down a narrow cutoff to drive the few miles to Ardmoyle. The census indicated we were to look for a two-windowed cottage—a place smaller than my grandfather's. We drove up and down the road but couldn't locate a cottage that matched the description on the census. Most of the cottages from the early 1700s were still standing, but there was no trace of the Beirne cottage.

I spied an old man leaning on his gate and smoking a pipe, and I asked Phil to stop the car. Pulling out a copy of the census, I approached him and asked if he could help. He placed his pipe on the fencepost and he picked up the document. He remembered a Beirne family, not my grandmother, of course, but the family of Patrick Beirne. He asked if Patrick could have been related to my grandmother? I knew that my grandmother had two brothers who emigrated to America; their names were Daniel and Patrick. The ship information indicated that Daniel Beirne traveled with my grandmother to Chicago; Patrick had sponsored them. Could Patrick have returned to Ireland? My grandmother never mentioned brothers. Had they returned just as Maggie had?

The old man introduced himself as Tom O'Dwyer; he showed me his family name on the census. I learned that seventy years ago he married a girl with the last name of Plunkett; her family name was on the census, as well. I was amazed at how little things had changed since the early 1900s. Many of the people were still living in the cottages of their ancestors. Mr. O'Dwyer told me the townland of Ardmoyle was changing. People from England were coming into the area and buying up the land and cottages. He pointed to the place next door and told us that a British lady had recently moved in. Putting his pipe between his crusty, weathered lips, he said he hoped we would find our Beirne family.

It was getting late and we were hungry. We had found out so much about my family, more than we ever hoped, but we still had lots of work to do in the short time we would be in Boyle. But for now, a good place to eat and a good night's sleep sounded like the perfect solution for our weary, hungry selves.

As we drove back into Boyle, I couldn't help but think of the wonderful treasures that might be inside my grandfather's cottage, and I hoped we could find Tom Cleary.

CHAPTER 11

This One's for You, Maggie

I had trouble sleeping. Something bothered me about my encounter with Liam McCarthy, yesterday. It was unsettling. The old man felt pretty comfortable taking liberties with a tourist—not only a tourist but also a relative of the Healy family. Liam's behavior surprised me, considering the history surrounding our families. Had I experienced a bit of the McCarthy charade? Maggie had suffered unhappiness because of her encounter with an aggressive McCarthy man. Am I to think that the McCarthy men are still badly behaved?

I wondered if Liam was related to Johnny. He hadn't responded to my question about that relationship. He heard me but stubbornly refused to answer. From my calculations, Liam was born in 1911, and I knew that Johnny was born in 1908. Could they be cousins? Did one of Liam's uncles impregnate Maggie? I wondered if these questions would ever be answered.

Johnny's birth certificate wasn't available from the County Office of Roscommon. That was unusual, since by

1908 all rural births were registered, and that left me wondering whether or not Johnny's birth was ever documented. The parish priest did baptize Johnny, but his baptism was an occasion of shame, rather than one of celebration. Nowhere on Johnny's baptismal record did the last name McCarthy appear, and I wondered if the McCarthy man ever really loved Maggie? Then I wondered if romance played any part in her life. Marriage was considered a commercial enterprise, rather than an affair of the heart, and affection didn't enter into the question of matrimony. Maggie's father was well into his nineties when she was of the age to marry; he couldn't offer a potential groom a dowry and with nothing to offer, Maggie had no chance of ever being married. Rather than being an embarrassing situation, maybe Maggie's pregnancy provided her with the only opportunity to ever have a child.

At breakfast the next morning, I mentioned my thoughts to Phil about Maggie and the McCarthy man. He listened carefully and agreed that Liam was indeed a very strange man and thought a McCarthy man, much like Liam, might have taken advantage of Maggie. With those final thoughts, we packed up our documents and headed back to Carrowkeel in search of Tom Cleary and to Bridie's cottage for the picture of Johnny.

Our familiarity with the Boyle area reassured us; Phil had a good grasp of the roads by now. Leaving the bustling village of Boyle behind, we entered the serene countryside. Rain threatened, but for now the sun peeked out through the gray clouds that hovered overhead. Rolling green meadows, sparkling with fresh dew, dipped into golden valleys. Small trees and thick shrubs clustered alongside the roads sheltered the wild hare and provided a sanctuary for the many species of birds. The winds blew strong against the brittle branches of the thorn bushes. Except for the few chipmunks that scurried across the gravel, the roads were deserted.

We parked across from Tom's cottage—or what we believed to be his cottage. The rope stretched across the driveway hadn't been removed, and the house still looked deserted. Phil and I walked to the rear of the cottage to see if anyone was working in the back. Not a soul was around, so we returned to the car.

A gray Honda sedan blew past us, breaking the silence of the quiet countryside. We wished that we had been able to get the driver's attention to ask if, indeed, we were at Tom Cleary's cottage. Luckily, we were about to get our wish because the driver turned around. The man behind the wheel looked familiar. As he pulled closer, we were surprised to see it was Liam. Since he wasn't getting out of his car, we walked over to him. He slowly rolled his window down, staring at us all the while. His eyes were glazed over. Something wasn't right about him. He acted as though he'd never met us before. Phil asked if he remembered us. Responding angrily that of course he did, he then got out of his car and asked me if I remembered yesterday's kiss. Not waiting for my answer, he demanded that we do it again. Then he told me he wanted to pat my backside while Phil took the picture. I was completely surprised by his request; yet, I couldn't help but laugh out loud at such a ridiculous proposition. Liam certainly was a very strange old man. Was he stalking me? Had I experienced a little of what Maggie might have felt? I wondered if she had anyone to protect her, for who would have believed her? The McCarthy name was well known in Boyle. Their homes were large, and they lived more comfortably than most people. Who would have believed the word of a poor farmer's daughter against the word of a rich man?

Before I had the chance to answer Liam, another car approached. The driver and passenger smiled and waved when they passed. I asked Liam if he knew them; he said he didn't. Then I asked Liam if we were at Tom's cottage. He looked past us and nodded. We asked where Tom could be, but Liam didn't answer. Instead, he pointed to our camera and insisted that Phil take a picture of us. Phil told him we had enough pictures. Not satisfied, he stood next to me with his hand poised for the butt pat. I moved away, reminding him that we had enough pictures. Then, I asked him if he was any relation to Johnny Healy. He said, "No." There was frustration in my voice; talking to Liam was a huge waste of time. We asked him once more if Tom lived in the cottage across from where we stood. He looked down at his dusty boots, and when he looked up, he pointed to the cottage next door. Annoyed, we turned, scrambled into our car, and drove off. If we never saw him again it would be fine with us. Although Liam didn't provide us with information about his relationship to Johnny, I knew the truth. It was as if I could feel it deep inside of me.

Tom's cottage looked tiny from the road because it was set way back into the pasture. We could see that his cottage was an exact replica of my grandfather's place, except that Tom's cottage had been updated. Painted a soft yellow with bright red geraniums planted in boxes on the windowsills, the cottage looked like a picture on a postcard. If it weren't for the storm clouds blocking the sun and casting a shadow, Tom's place would have been perfect for the cover of the Travel Ireland magazine.

The rain began to fall as we ran to the door. A woman immediately opened it and ushered us inside. I asked her if she knew Tom Cleary. She introduced herself as Colleen, his wife. Phil and I sighed with relief. Then we shed our jackets and wiped our shoes on the mat.

Seated comfortably in their parlor, I showed Colleen the 1901 Irish Census and told her that I was Johnny Healy's second cousin. She couldn't believe that we came all the way from Chicago to find the old cottage. Assuring us that Tom would be home at any time, she began to tell us about Johnny and how he died. "Tom had always been very good to Johnny" she began, "helping him around the farm, taking him to town to shop, and driving him to the Post to pick up his pension check every month." Tom had taken Johnny to the hospital the day he became too ill to remain alone in the cottage. Johnny had asked Tom and Colleen to promise they would take him out of the hospital, so he could die at their cottage, rather than the sterile environment of a care facility. When the time did come, Tom brought Johnny to their cottage. Colleen remembered Johnny's last breath. She said, "It was as if the wind passed through him, and he left with the breeze." The neighbors dug the grave, the wake was held at the Cleary cottage, and Johnny was laid to rest in the Killarght Graveyard with his mother and all of his ancestors.

Colleen was surprised to learn that we had already visited the graveyard and commented on our amazing ability to find our way around in such a short time. Then she asked who we were talking to by the side of the road. Both she and her daughter-in-law had been shopping and were worried when they saw our cars pulled off the road. We told her that Liam McCarthy helped us find her cottage and asked if she knew him? She knew him all right, and I could tell from the tone of her voice that she didn't care much for him. Colleen told us that Liam and Johnny were first cousins. Liam never attended Johnny's funeral, and she verified the fact that Johnny had lived his life in the shadow of the McCarthy family.

Colleen told us that the McCarthy man who impregnated Maggie left for America shortly after. He knew that Maggie was pregnant, and he still left. When Johnny was born, it was standard practice for an illegitimate baby to be taken away from its mother and placed into an orphanage. When the child reached the age of sixteen, he or she would be put out into the streets with only the clothes they wore. It didn't matter where they went, for they had no family. Many of them turned to begging or they took passage to England to earn a living. Johnny had been fortunate. The Healy family made a decision that was unprecedented among the rural Irish Catholics. Maggie's father welcomed the baby into their home and gave him the name Healy. Colleen then asked that we not talk to anyone in the McCarthy family, out of respect for Johnny. I understood, but felt I had already blemished his memory by talking to Liam. Worse yet, I had allowed him to kiss me. Feeling ill, I asked Colleen for a glass of water.

Colleen looked out the front window and told us that Tom must be trying to get the cows in out of the storm. She asked us to put on our shoes and grab our coats; she would drive us to him. We piled into her small car, and when she switched on the engine, the twang of American country music filled the air. Colleen, seeing my surprised look, told me how much she preferred American music.

She drove down the side roads and turned into a pasture. We bumped and banged our way up the mud path and stopped in front of a barn. Colleen left, telling us to stay put. After a few minutes, a man appeared at my window. Wait a minute! I knew that man; I met him on the road yesterday. He was the large man in the small car in back of our "cow parade." Rolling my window down, I heard Tom tell Colleen, "These are the people I told you about yesterday—the impatient tourists in back of the herd."

We both laughed while he extended his hand into the car to shake mine. Then Tom asked who we were. I told him my maiden name was Shea and that we came to find my grandfather's cottage on Carrowkeel. He stepped back in surprise and said, "You are from the Shea family in America? Johnny told me the Shea family would visit from America one day and when they arrived, they were to see the cottage."

My cheeks felt damp, and I thought that maybe it was the raindrops that wet my face, or maybe not.

Tom told Colleen to take us back to their cottage; he would follow soon after he finished tending the herd. On our drive back up the road, Colleen talked about the strange coincidence of meeting Tom on the road and finding him again in the pasture. I could hear both Colleen and Phil talking and laughing. Nothing I could say would have been heard, for my heart sang in celebration!

We hurried into the Cleary cottage to wait for Tom. Colleen listened to the story of how we came to learn about Johnny. I showed her pictures of my grandfather and my mother, who was Johnny's first cousin. She said how sad we hadn't come sooner. Johnny didn't like very many people, but she was sure he would have liked us. Colleen placed the teakettle on the stove and then reached for the china cups that hung from a beautifully carved breakfront.

Suddenly the wind pushed its way into the parlor, and we heard the door slam. Tom arrived just in time for tea and to warm his cold hands by the fire. Colleen placed a load of peat into the hearth and it blazed its warmth throughout the room. While we sipped our tea, Tom settled into the big chair by the fire. His thick blonde hair lay flattened to his head in the shape of his wool cap. His cheeks had a rosy glow from the strong winds and sleet he had been working in. I noticed his large calloused hands holding the delicate teacup very carefully between his thick fingers. I pictured Tom with a huge mug of steaming hot coffee, not a delicate china cup filled with mint tea. I smiled at that mental picture. I was grateful to be in the Cleary cottage with people who had known the Healy family.

Colleen told us their cottage had been in her family for over 200 years. She knew Peter Healy since she was a little girl. She remembered him as being very kind to children. She knew Johnny, too. He was the skilled handyman in the area; in fact, he had completed the remodeling work on their cottage. It was beautifully done. A parlor had been added, and all the rooms had been rehabbed. Linoleum covered the floors. The cottage was cozy, but we noticed the area away from the fire had a damp feel to it. We pulled our chairs closer to the hearth, enjoying its warmth, as well as the hot tea and good company.

Tom welcomed the opportunity to tell stories about Ireland. He explained how life was eighty years ago, when his father was a young man. There was no decimal currency; in fact, there was no system of weights and measurements. The average pay for a worker was three pounds, ten shillings a week, and luxuries were scarce.

Tom and Colleen were in their late fifties. When they were growing up, the cinema cost three pounds and ice cream sold for four shillings. Indoor bathrooms were unheard of, and they remembered all too well the cold days and nights going out to the fields to relieve themselves. When indoor plumbing was introduced, the old people would have none of it. They thought it would make the house damp. There was no refrigeration. Meat, milk, and butter had to be kept in a cold place in the house, or else outside. Laundry was washed in galvanized tubs, and that same tub was used for the weekly baths drawn up in front of the hearth on Saturday nights.

Johnny lived in that old world. He didn't have an indoor bathroom until a couple of years before he died and, as far as anyone knew, he hadn't a proper bath in years. Johnny read the weekly newspaper by the light of a bare bulb that hung from the middle of his ceiling. Tom pointed to the lovely breakfront in his parlor. It was the same breakfront that Peter had hauled home one day from the fair, and Colleen remarked how out of place it had looked in his shabby old cottage. I remembered that story from Bridie.

It must have been quite an event that afternoon—one small donkey cart and one huge, over-sized breakfront. Peter and Johnny were very proud of that piece, for it held all their cookware, silverware, dishes, cups, and odds and ends. By the time Tom received it, after Johnny died, it needed a major overhauling. Tom knew it was worth quite a sum of money, once he had it refinished. We snapped some pictures to file away in the family album. Then Tom asked us if we would like to see the inside of my grandfather's cottage.

He said he would meet us there; he had some things to do first. We figured that was a good plan. It gave us time to pick up Johnny's picture from Bridie. Colleen and Tom had no pictures of him to give us.

Bridie was waiting for us at her door and asked us in for tea. We told her that we had found Tom and that he was going to let us in to see the cottage. She understood. She invited us to return another time and went into her kitchen to fetch the picture. When she handed it to me, I searched Johnny's image for any resemblance to my grandfather. Johnny was short and thin; he had a sweet face—just like my grandfather's. I placed the picture in my briefcase, and we said our good-byes, promising to stay in touch. I hoped that we hadn't seemed rude, but I was anxious to see the inside of my family's cottage.

Clouds gathered overhead, and we could smell rain off in the distance. Tom pulled up just then. He removed what looked to be a large box from the trunk of his car, and I saw that he was also holding a picture. He asked me to identify Peter Healy, who was somewhere in the crowd among his tug-of-war teammates. I picked him out immediately. He looked just like my grandfather. We never thought we'd ever see a picture of Peter Healy. Tom said that Johnny had told him to give that picture to the Shea family when they came from America. I still couldn't get over the fact that Johnny knew about us. Well, maybe not about all of us. My grandfather must have written to his family on Carrowkeel to tell them of his daughter Helen's marriage to my father, Mike Shea. He must have been proud to write that letter. To think that Johnny remembered the name of Shea really meant something to me!

Then Tom showed us the key to the front door and asked if we were ready to go inside.

CHAPTER 12

The Cottage

Tom took the lead. We followed him up the stone walk to the front door just as it began to drizzle. Thunder rumbled in the distance, mimicking the staccato sounds of a drum roll. The old key clinked against the metal plate. Tom pushed on the heavy wooden door and it creaked open. Immediately, the acrid smell of mildew seeped out. As if in ceremony, Phil and Tom stepped aside and motioned me to proceed. I waited for my eyes to adjust to the darkness before venturing into the gloomy hallway of the abandoned cottage, overwhelmed by the lingering aromas of the generations of Healy families who had gone before me.

We teetered over construction planks. Tom apologized for the mess, saying they were using the place for storage. Balancing myself on stacks of two-by-fours, I identified each of the small dark rooms off the hallway. I knew the layout of the interior—it was exactly like Bridie's cottage.

I rounded the corner and entered the kitchen. The room was untouched, and I was relieved to hear that nothing had been removed from it since Johnny's death.

The linoleum had curled at the corners and was cracked at the baseboards. Johnny had tossed various throw rugs down in an apparent attempt to add coziness, but they only absorbed moisture from the dampness. Particles of mold were everywhere. The walls were painted turquoise. There was a bulky iron peat stove similar to Bridie's, but it looked like it had never been used. Tom told us that Johnny disliked anything modern. The stove frustrated him, and besides, it didn't cook the food as well as the open hearth.

An ancient kitchen table, pushed under the window, served as the workbench and for dining, its ragged oilcloth runner stained the colors of the vegetables from Johnny's garden. A tiny sink embedded with years of dirt stuck out from the side of the wall; it supplied only cold water. The line was attached to a cistern outside that accumulated rainwater off the roof. When Johnny needed hot water, he boiled it, just as his family had always done. A heavy upholstered armchair faced the stove. I imagined that Johnny spent many lonely nights in that chair. His mother, Maggie, might have used it to rest after a day of toiling in the fields.

I felt alone in the deserted old cottage, even though Phil and Tom were present. A despairing hopelessness surrounded the place, and that feeling seeped into my troubled spirit. The cottage had been left untended far too long, and it made me sad to think its walls would never again resonate with the rich brogue of the Healys or be warmed by the peat that now lay stacked outside the back door. I heard Phil and Tom moving about, speaking softly, respectfully giving me my space.

A wobbly, rusted metal cabinet caught my eye. Its bent door hung partially open, and the soft colors of pretty spring flowers peeked out from the shadows. When I opened the door, three lovely teacups presented themselves. They were stacked atop sheets of yellowed newspaper. Grime and neglect couldn't dull the beauty of the china. It cheered me to think that Johnny, Peter, and Maggie owned a few items that reflected the good life.

Tom pointed to two pictures hanging near the hearth. One he knew for sure dated back to the 1800s, a picture of the Sacred Heart of Jesus. It hung from an old nail resembling a bolt, and the discolored, splintered wood frame was cracked and chipped. Tom climbed onto a rickety chair to retrieve it for me. The part of the wall behind the picture was smoky white—an obvious contrast to the dark turquoise wall. Tom handed me the picture, and I noticed a charred plywood board attached to the back of it. The picture looked as though it had been in a fire. Blackened and stained, it reeked of smoke. The smell was strong, as if the peat fire were still burning. Streaks of moisture marred the front. I read the saying that was written onto the picture: I will bless the house in which the image of my Sacred Heart shall be exposed and honored, and I will give peace in their families. I wondered if that promise had been kept for those who lived in this little cottage. Had the Sacred Heart protected my family's kindred souls? And did those blessings also follow the young emigrants to America? Tom retrieved another picture from the wall opposite the hearth, a lovely scene of an English cottage. It could barely be seen through smoke-encrusted glass. Mold saturated the picture frame, and tiny bugs infested the paper backing. I guessed that Johnny had carried the picture back from England, where he worked for five years before the war.

I sat at the large hearth and imagined the sounds of family. My great-grandfather and his father before him had sat by this same hearth to plan which fields to till or, perhaps, to prepare to assist in the delivery of a calf. My great-grandmother smoothed her weathered hands over her bulging belly, yet another baby to add to the blessings of a large family. My grandfather, as a small boy, played and studied by its flickering light. Sweet sounds of babies cooing, celebrations of bountiful harvests, moans of hunger, and anguished cries once filled these rooms. When the potato rotted, it was in this room the hopes and dreams for the good life had evaporated. Now a barrier of concrete silences the hearth—its spirits locked away, forever.

I peeled away a corner of the rotting linoleum and touched the cold stone floor. "My dear grandfather," I whispered, "I have come in order to feel your spirit, so that I may tell my daughter and her children about you. It was here in this humble cottage you were born and it was here you made the decision to leave for America. Do you have any idea the wonderful legacy you have bestowed on your children and your grandchildren—the opportunity to live and prosper in America?"

Crossing the cramped hallway, I entered the bedroom belonging to my great-grandparents. I ran my hands along the rough stone wall. A small peat fireplace half hidden by a dilapidated dresser caught my eye. Ashes and chunks of peat were piled on top of an iron grate; the back wall was blackened from generations of fires. Images of my great-grandmother spinning wool, mending clothes, and falling exhausted into bed each night flashed through my mind. I closed my eyes for a moment to block out the gloom of the cold, gray afternoon. My fingers traced the cracked tiles around the hearth. On top of the dusty, smoky mantelpiece were two lovely delicate delft china vases. The dampness had laid claim to their finish, and tiny cracks marred the blue and white pattern. Tom's soft voice brought me back to the moment. Standing behind me, he told me I could have those vases because he knew how much they meant to Maggie. I gently lifted each one, being very thankful for Tom's generosity.

I carried them to the kitchen and placed them on the table. The items I collected lay like treasures on the faded tablecloth. The small china dog that I spied yesterday from outside the window looked lonely keeping sentry on the thick windowsill; I slipped it into my pocket for safekeeping.

Phil asked about a pipe that was suspended from the ceiling in the kitchen. Tom explained it was part of the original gas lamp installed in the early 1900s. Next to that pipe hung an electrical cord supporting a lone bulb. There were no other lights in the cottage, and the only electrical outlet in the entire place was in the kitchen. Phil and Tom discussed safety issues while I wandered around, trying to imagine how my grandfather survived without all the things I perceived as necessary for comfort.

I noticed a door at the other end of the hallway, and I left the kitchen to investigate. The bolts were rusted, difficult to move. I jiggled the knobs and pushed on the door. With one good shove, it swung open. A concrete barn was directly in front of me, about twenty feet away. Defined as an outbuilding on the census, the barn looked exactly like the cottage, the same length and width. The doors no more than five feet four inches tall, matched those inside the cottage. Divided into three tiny areas, the barn could accommodate only one horse, one cow, and one pig. The ever-present aroma of livestock mixed with the musty smell of peat must have been overwhelming, especially in the summer. I wondered how soundly anyone slept at night with the animals so close to the bedroom window.

I walked around outside, careful not to wander too far because the dark sky threatened rain. The roofs were covered in gray asphalt shingles. Thatched roofs were prevalent until the 1970s. It was easier to tile the roof with shingles, which looked neater and proved to be more cost efficient. The thatch would have carried debris into the living area of the cottage, causing moisture and pollen to accumulate on the walls and floors. With the continuous burning of peat and the smelly thatch that hung overhead, it's amazing the Irish weren't more prone to lung disorders. The night skies were moving in, and soon we wouldn't be able to see without the aid of a flashlight. The sound of thunder chased me back inside. With more to investigate, I drifted into Johnny's bedroom, which had a twin bed pushed up against the wall. A wobbly toilet and makeshift shower had been recently installed. The waste emptied out the side of the cottage and into an underground pit.

Johnny never had a telephone, and he never learned to drive. He rode an old bicycle wherever he went. It was only a few years before he died that he stopped cycling into Boyle. His uncle Peter had a donkey and a cart, and he also rode a bicycle. Tom had tried to bring the modern world into Johnny's cottage, but Johnny would have none of it. The cottage had no electricity until the late 1980s. Though someone had given him a radio, and Tom had introduced a television in 1993, Johnny refused to use any modern conveniences and complained about their intrusion. There were no closets and no place to store extra clothing or shoes. Then I reminded myself that there were no extras in the lives of these people. They wore out what they had and then figured out how to replace it.

Tom waited for us outside while Phil and I walked through the cottage one last time. We gathered the items we had collected and carried them to the car. The rain stopped, giving us time to store them safely on the back-seat. To the casual observer we may have looked like junk haulers, but I was intent on preserving priceless family treasures. Through them, the lives of my family in Ireland came alive to us. We found what we came in search of— the cottage of the Healy family. If only we could locate the cottage of my grandmother Sarah Beirne from Ardmoyle. But that wasn't possible; it was gone. There seemed to be no trace of my Beirne family.

We invited Tom and his wife to dinner at a pub in town. They accepted and suggested we meet them in Boyle at six o'clock. The minute we closed our car doors, the skies opened up again and the rain poured down. From all the rain that had fallen since our arrival, I was convinced that Ireland would one day float away.

We hurried to our bed and breakfast to freshen up. I wrapped the pictures from the cottage in newspaper and rolled the vases in my shirts. I tried to fit as much as I could into my suitcase for safekeeping.

Tom and Colleen arrived at the pub just after six. We preferred the fancy menu—it seemed the most appropriate way to celebrate our successful journey. The kitchen was closed for the evening but, luckily, Colleen's sister worked at the pub, and they agreed to serve us. We spent the evening chatting and feasting on a traditional Irish meal of homemade vegetable soup with brown bread and good Irish beef with lots of potatoes. Tom and Colleen were pleasant and caring individuals. It was easy to see why Johnny cared so much for them.

I asked Tom what the night was like in the countryside of Boyle with no streetlights, street signs, or road markings. Tom laughed and suggested we drive to the cottage and park in front to see for ourselves. Right then, Phil and I decided to do just that.

After saying our good-byes and promising to write, we climbed into our car and drove out of Boyle toward Carrowkeel. The storms had moved out to sea, and the sky was filled with millions of white twinkling stars. When we arrived at my grandfather's cottage, we were overwhelmed by the night and silenced by the calm. There was not a leaf rustling, an animal scurrying, or the chirp of a cricket. The sweet aroma from a neighbor's peat fire drifted toward us but was quickly diverted by the shifting winds. I could have stayed there forever, for it was so peaceful. Our eyes eventually adjusted to the dark, and the mystery of the night sky was revealed. Clusters of twinkling bright lights and distant galaxies came into view. A transparent strip of white banded across the sky; the Milky Way seemed to float, balancing planets closest to the earth. The brilliance of Venus lit up the heavens while the fading Mars remained a fixture, unable to compete with the glistening stars that surrounded it. Light from the full moon illuminated the cottage.

My grandfather had left this tranquil country setting to live in a grimy, industrial city in America. How he must have missed the beauty and the unbelievable peace and restful solitude. How did he ever make the adjustment? On nights when he sat on his porch in Chicago, did he dream of Carrowkeel? I know that I will.

The kitchen in my grandfather's Cottage   2004

My great-grandfather's bedroom in the cottage—the rooms are very small   2004

Town of Boyle, County Roscommon, Ireland

Road to the Townland of Carrowkeel, Boyle

My grandfather's brother Peter Healy taken with his tug of war team in Boyle   1920s

Johnny Healy   1995

My grandfather's cottage on Carrowkeel, Boyle, County Roscommon, Ireland

The barn behind the cottage—each small door opened to reveal a space just large enough to house one animal each

St. Bridget's Church in Boyle, County Roscommon—the Healy and Beirne family church

A typical country Irish road

CHAPTER 13

Michael Shea
Cahersiveen,
County Kerry, Ireland

1867-1869

The town was embroiled in political uprisings. Tempers flared as young Kerry Freedom Fighters organized to overthrow the British government. When Michael was eight years old, he overheard his father and the neighbors talking about fighting the English to gain their freedom. Michael admired his father's bravery, and even though he was too young to join their crusade, he championed the cause.

In 1872 when Michael turned thirteen, the Home Rule Party convinced the Irish that they deserved the right to govern themselves. These were dangerous times for the determined Irish who wanted only to break free of British rule; any careless move could result in death or imprisonment.

The winter of 1878-79 was a difficult one; famine loomed over Ireland. Harsh weather and recurring blight caused the potato to rot, and excessively cold, wet weather spread livestock diseases and destroyed cash crops. Michael witnessed destitute neighbors forced to leave their cottages for the shelter of the poorhouse, where they were sure to die from exposure and starvation.

There was no end to the hopelessness and sorrow of everyday life, and if Michael ever intended to marry, he couldn't stay in Ireland. Because he had no land and no promise of a farm, no father would be willing to give him his daughter. He'd remain a bachelor, referred to as a "boy" to the townspeople for all of his life. And with that distinction, he would live a shamed existence with his parents or married brothers, a second-class family member in crowded quarters. Michael decided he had to emigrate.

Stories circulated among the townspeople about those who had fared well in the New World. Michael listened with great interest, for he knew about agents from various shipping lines offering passage to America to anyone willing to build new cities. America offered a bright beacon— a paradise of liberty and opportunity. He couldn't tell whether he felt happy or sad when he thought of leaving Cahersiveen, but one thing he did know: without food in his belly, he could have no feelings in his heart or thoughts in his head of missing Ireland.

CHAPTER 14

Michael's Emigration

August 1880

Michael squinted at the sunrays settling on his weathered face. Slate dust drifted to his shoulders and gathered in the folds of his shirt. His hand-sewn boots, covered in gray powder, were worn thin at the tops, and the soles were desperate for repair. Michael walked the four miles from his family's cottage in Cahersiveen to Renard Point to board the ferry to Valentia Island; from there, he walked two more miles to the quarry. He worked eleven hours a day, six days a week.

He knew poverty and hard work. His wages at the slate quarry were paid in yellow meal instead of money. If there were another failure of the potato crop, money would be of no use, since there would be no food to buy. Work at the quarry was not only backbreaking but also dangerous. Gunpowder and strong hands helped to shift the slate out of its position, and cranes suspended from the roof of the quarry hoisted the large slabs into wagons for the two-mile journey to the slate yard in Knightstown.

Michael noticed the tiny pieces of slate that had worked their way beneath the skin of his large, calloused hands and the flakes of stone and mud under all his fingernails. His elbows were scraped, and his arms carried the scars from chips of slate.

After church on Sundays, Michael walked to the Crossroads for an afternoon of socializing and dance. When he was not needed at home, he spent time in the company of his good friends.

During the summer, Irish youth were summoned from the Crossroads to welcome the British gentry. A fiddler seated on a three-legged stool began the merriment with a reel and, little by little, everyone joined in the jig. Michael danced as though there was no tomorrow, stomping his feet on the stage, breaking into a sweat, and forgetting, at least for the moment, his troubles.

The opportunity to emigrate presented itself, and Michael was ready. In August 1880, he signed an "X" onto a contract obliging him to work for a road-building firm in the State of Connecticut. For the price of a steerage ticket, Michael agreed to work five years for a salary of four dollars per week. He set about packing his things: one towel, two pair of socks, one cap, one suit of clothes, and a muffler. Placing the items on his blanket, he bundled it and fastened it tightly with twine.

A farewell supper or "feast of departure" was held for each emigrant before they left on their journey. Also known as the "American Wake," it signified a death, for the loved one departing was as good as dead to the family. Friends and family watched over them in order to prevent evil spirits from entering their souls.

Michael spent his last evening in Cahersiveen at his farewell wake. A professional keener (an old woman of the parish noted for her ability to wail and lament) knelt in the corner and began her lament after Michael's final jig with his brothers. The keener enumerated Michael's virtues and grieved for the family's loss and sorrow. At dawn, the guests stepped outside so that the family could bid their last farewells in private. Torment webbed the air and emotions made it difficult to breathe and talk. When Michael was released from his family's embrace, they knew they might never see or talk to each other again.

Michael promised to send them money for their passage to America, but only a miracle would take them there, and it was clear there were no miracles for the Shea family—only hard work and suffering.

Michael walked the sixty miles to Killarney, where he boarded the train to Queenstown—the large harbor in Cork city. When he arrived at the pier, he was surprised to see the noisy hawkers selling pots, combs, oatcakes, and turf for deck fires. Emigrants jammed the dock; everyone and everything was inspected and de-loused. Michael gagged from the irritating spray. Thousands of people lined the pier to board the tenders. Michael's ship, The Arizona, hadn't yet posted its sailing date, and he was told to return in the morning for any news of its scheduled departure.

He stored his luggage at the pier and looked for accommodations. Luckily, the first place he found offered bed and breakfast for two shillings per night. When he opened the door to the room, he was discouraged to see five men crowded into one small bed and many others sleeping on the floor. He was told that as many as twenty-six men had been known to lie on the floor in a space no more than seventeen feet long by ten feet wide. Squeezing himself onto the bed, he fell into a fitful sleep.

Around midnight, he was startled awake by the brisk music of fiddles and pipes. Traveling musicians played their instruments in order to encourage those sleeping on the bed to jump up and dance. The men on the floor took that opportunity to crowd into the bed. Michael easily fell victim to this scheme. Dance was his passion.

The next morning, after a feast of tea and bread, he walked to the crowded pier with hopes of boarding his ship. The next day he joined the queue on the docks again. Finally, on the third day, the company announced that the Arizona, bound for America, was loading its passengers.

Michael joined the others filing onto steerage deck—the area of the ship reserved for the poor. Over one thousand emigrants jammed the deck, pressing forward with anxious anticipation.

The Irish Protestants booked themselves into first and second-class accommodations. They could afford such luxury because the British government generously rewarded them for giving up their Catholic faith. Dressed in their finery, they stood glaring down at their fellow Irishmen crowding into steerage and, raising their wine glasses, drank to the wise decision of becoming Protestants. Michael felt pity for them. Feeling sad and somewhat discouraged, he remained on deck until the last little spot of the coast of Ireland faded from sight.

The days and nights spent in steerage were not for the faint of heart. Overcrowding, unsanitary conditions, poor treatment, along with insufficient food and narrow berths plagued the weary passengers. Seasickness, resulting from the maddening storms and jagged ghostly icebergs provided the inspiration for their desperate prayers. Michael had heard horror stories about the journey to America before the famine of 1847,when the voyage took six to eight weeks. Now, in 1880, the Arizona cut swiftly through the heavy water like a sword, promising a short journey of eight days.

Inclement weather kept Michael and the other steerage passengers locked inside their dark, damp prison-like environment. Murky water reached out from the turbulent sea, crashing onto the deck of the rolling ship, and gale-force winds whistled above their heads. Pounding rain and hail sounded as if nails had been dumped onto the deck above their heads, while the shifting cargo stowed beneath steerage banged at the walls. Muffled voices of the burly crew could be heard overhead, and screams of frightened children and terrified women echoed throughout the ship. The hold was a treacherous place. Whenever a violent storm erupted, half the bunks crashed to the floor, and water poured in.

The fear of being shipwrecked, along with thoughts of a watery grave, kept Michael awake for most of the journey. On good days, a fiddler's tune could be heard coming from the deck, and for a few moments Michael was back in Ireland, dancing at the Crossroads.

When the Arizona entered New York harbor, throngs of passengers crowded the deck. American inspectors climbed on board to check the passengers for signs of disease. Michael watched as the first and second-class passengers were treated to tea and biscuits while they waited for their physical exams. White-gloved officers escorted the privileged, and it took two days to empty the ship of the elite. The barges finally arrived to load the steerage passengers. Michael was careful not to limp, squint, or scratch for fear that he might be pulled out of line for further inspection. His journey had caused him a tremendous amount of anxiety. The physical discomfort of the cramped, smelly quarters of the steerage compartment had overwhelmed him.

Once inside Castle Gardens, long lines of immigrants waiting to be processed snaked through the narrow corridors, spilling out into the main hall. Each steerage passenger was inspected for mental defects, back problems, conjunctivitis, trachoma, lameness, goiters, pregnancy, and eye problems. The unsuspecting few who showed signs of physical or mental problems were marked with chalk, pulled from the line and re-inspected.

Michael stood for hours waiting for the one doctor on duty to perform the routine exam and was grateful to finally gain approval to enter America. His bundle had been dumped into the baggage room where exhausted passengers sorted through the piles to locate their belongings. Many of the bags had been opened or destroyed and articles stolen by the unscrupulous few who roamed the area. Beyond the baggage department was an unpaved yard, where families already in America came to collect their weary families and friends. Those with no one to claim them either paid their own train passage to other parts of the country or wandered into New York City to join the thousands of other barely surviving immigrants.

The young man stood alone in the crowd. His clothing was wrinkled and soiled. Around his neck hung a tag identifying him as an immigrant contract worker. Jobs as day laborers and servants were being handed out, but not as freely to the Irish, who were considered too contentious to be good employees. Many companies hung signs that read "Irish Need Not Apply." Michael showed the agent his contract to work in a state whose name he couldn't pronounce. Forms were left blank because Michael didn't understand the questions, nor could he provide an address. The officer ushered him to the train platform, handed him a small parcel of food, and secured him a ticket to New London, Connecticut.

Michael watched out the window of the train as the scenery flashed by. With a ticket clutched tightly in his hand, his thoughts strayed to Cahersiveen and the life he had left behind. Straightening his shoulders and lifting his chin, he saw in the window a face he barely recognized. Haggard and drawn, his features seemed as foreign to him as the landscape.

The fresh air rushing through the open window kept Michael alert, while the steady movement of the train soothed his jittery nerves. He dreamed of the Kerry dance when he danced himself into frenzy with the lovely Valentia women. He wondered if people danced in Connecticut, and if so, could they dance the jig?

The train continued on to New London, crowded with the immigrants. Determination and perseverance replaced the sadness etched on Michael's face, as well as on the faces of his fellow travelers. He looked forward to saving enough money to send to Ireland so that his family could join him sometime soon. Already he was lonely for their companionship.

CHAPTER 15

Michael Settles in New London, Connecticut

September 1880-1882

His accommodations were barely tolerable. The springs from Michael's iron bed poked through the wafer-thin mattress. His nights were distressingly sleepless. The tattered wallpaper hung loose in the corners where moisture gathered from a leak in the roof. One of the broken glass panes invited torrents of water to rain in on the sagging bed closest to the window. Luckily, Michael's iron cot was pushed up against the corner next to the entrance. If he cracked the splintered door just a bit, it provided a draft that cooled him on hot, sticky nights. The smell of spoiled fish permeated the air, and there was no escaping the odor of rotted garbage that hung thick between the ramshackle buildings.

The tenement flat smelled of foreign cooking and the unwashed flesh of its inhabitants. Michael missed the fresh sea air that filtered through the drafty cottage in Ireland. He recalled the sweet smell of peat and the rich earth aroma of thatch that provided the comfort with which to weave his nightly dreams.

Raucous screams of husbands and wives beating on each other echoed through the narrow, dirty hallway. Children ran half-naked down the cramped stairwell and onto the street. Stray dogs rooted through garbage, searching for scraps left behind by beggars.

Despite all its shortcomings, the tenement on Harbor Street was safer than the streets, where criminals lurked. Michael learned a painful lesson two nights after his arrival, when his pockets were picked clean in a dark alley.

Michael shared one room with five other Irishmen who had arrived in New London a few months before him. They were friendly enough but teased Michael about the way he saved his hard-earned money. The men were older and had seen their share of barroom brawls and nights spent in dark alleys sleeping off a binge. They nagged him like old fish-women, urging him to join them for a pint or two on a Saturday night, but Michael remained staunch in his resolve to save money from his meager wages. He worked twelve-hour days, six days a week, digging ditches and hauling cement to construct roads and bridges. He had promised his family passage to America, and he had every intention of honoring that pledge.

He paid two dollars each week to a callous landlady who would sooner see the Irish sleeping in filthy gutters. Michael knew that hatred of anything or anyone Irish seeped into every corner of New London. His breakfast and supper were included with the rent. Michael made sure to arrive at the breakfast table before the others, since he had once made the mistake of arriving late and finding little food, he went hungry for most of the day. His suppers were enough to fill him, but he longed for his mother's smoked meat and homemade brown bread spread with freshly churned butter.

The backbreaking work all week suppressed any desire to celebrate, but Saturday nights found everyone out in the streets. When Michael did stop to peek through the smoke-smeared windows of the saloons, the fancy women gathering inside made him feel uncomfortable. In Ireland, women weren't welcome at the pubs, nor would they even consider entering the male domain of a drinking establishment.

Michael and his roommates were vulnerable in the crime-ridden city and insecure in their ability to protect themselves against the thugs that roamed the waterfront. The danger of being robbed was ever present, not only on the streets of New London, but in the rooming house, where one skeleton key unlocked every door. Their jobs identified their low social status, and their poverty made them poor candidates for success.

Michael had no friends, no family, and no way out of his appalling poverty. He felt deluded by his fanciful visions of America. When he left Ireland, he carried nothing with him to remind him of home, no shamrock, piece of turf, or family photos. Now, sitting alone in his room, he felt homesick for anything Irish. His mind wandered across the Atlantic to the Kerry shore. He longed for companionship, a night of the Kerry dance, a good fiddler, and a piper to create the music that would spirit him away, if only for a few hours, from the unhappiness all around him.

There were many surprises in store for Michael. He expected only sunshine in America, but the oven-like air of a New London summer was a far cry from Ireland's perpetual dampness. Winters in America were harsh, with snow, freezing temperatures, and sleet. Michael spent some of his precious savings for a heavy wool jacket and long woolen underwear. His wool cap wasn't thick enough to keep his head warm, and his calloused hands were chapped by the blustery winds that whipped the Connecticut coast.

Thousands of immigrants flooded into New London from all parts of the world, and Michael began to realize the hopelessness of his life. After two years, he was no better off than when he first stepped foot on American soil.

Michael's involvement in the Catholic Church had waned with his arrival in America. He often arrived late for Sunday Mass and left before Communion. He hadn't confessed his sins to a priest since leaving Ireland, and enormous guilt crept into his empty soul. Michael blamed God and the church for his prolonged suffering, and those feelings served as a wedge to shatter his faith.

As long as Michael felt obligated to attend Sunday Mass, it might as well be in the grandest church in New London. The parish of St. Mary, Star of the Sea was the largest church in New London. Sitting on a hill overlooking the Thames River, it was built in 1871 and regarded as one of the most impressive churches in the area. Paintings commissioned by the Vatican hung on the walls between the Stations of the Cross, and the stained glass windows were renowned for their rich colors.

One crisp December Sunday morning, Michael bumped into the parish priest while hurrying down the aisle to the freedom of the streets. Father Sheehan understood that Michael was a frightened, haunted young man who looked worse than some of the beggars who roamed the streets of the city. He had noticed Michael on other Sundays, arriving late and leaving early.

Father Sheehan greeted Michael in the Irish language. Avoiding his eyes, Michael moved around the priest in search of the door. The good priest laid his hand on Michael's arm and asked to walk with him. Michael was surprised but thankful for the company. It had been a long time since he had spoken with anyone about his family in Ireland or shared his passionate yearning for a glimpse of the enchanted mountains that surrounded his beloved Cahersiveen. The walk with Father Sheehan was good for Michael's troubled spirit, and he felt at peace for the first time in a long time.

Michael told Father Sheehan about the rat-infested tenement where he lived, his painful labors with the road building crew, and his aching memories of the Kerry dance. That was the beginning of a friendship that allowed Michael to let down his guard, and he asked the priest for help in sending money to Ireland for his family's passage to America. Father Sheehan generously offered his assistance and more.

Interested in Michael's love of the music and the jig, the priest invited him to the Saturday night dances held at St. Patrick's Church in Norwich, just ten miles away. In fact, if Michael agreed to help teach the dance, Father Sheehan promised to provide the horse cart to deliver him to St. Patrick's. Michael jumped at the opportunity. When a smile spread across Michael's face, the priest felt assured that he had recruited a valuable addition to their struggling parish events.

Those Saturday nights spent at St. Patrick's were Michael's happiest times in America. The good priest provided him with a new suit and fine leather boots for dancing. Michael stored his new clothes at the church because he knew they would disappear from the crowded room he shared on Harbor Street.

He spent hours teaching the dance to the young Irish men and women of St. Patrick's parish. He dominated the dance floor with poise and confidence. His broad shoulders moved easily with the rhythm of the piper, and the young Irish women began to notice the young man who performed the dance as if he had a fire raging in his boots.

Michael asked Father Sheehan if he would send remittances to Ireland for him. While the priest wrote the letter, Michael unpinned the money from inside his ragged sock. With trembling hands, Michael counted out each dollar. Proud to have saved such an appreciable amount, he handed Father Sheehan the forty dollars that would purchase ship tickets, as well as train fare when the time came. It had taken Michael two years to save that money—all for this moment!

Michael waited impatiently for a response. Father Sheehan promised that the minute word arrived, he would make sure to get the message to him. Michael thought of his beloved mother and father and how happy he'd be to see them; he trusted the good priest would help them find a clean and affordable place to live.

Word arrived two months later. Father Sheehan himself rushed to the tenement on Harbor Street with the letter. Michael's ice-cold fingers couldn't find the thin edge of the envelope. He blew on his hands and cupped them between his knees to thaw them. His big, clumsy fingers tore at the paper. The minute he pulled the printed pages from the envelope, he handed them to Father Sheehan.

The letter began with the news of his parents' deaths. The priest continued reading, but Michael, shocked by the startling news, fell back onto his bed. His parents, Julia and Michael, had died within two months of each other, one year ago. Tears rolled down his face, finding their way into the lines that had formed around his mouth. He had aged since he left Ireland, and no amount of tears would heal his wounded heart. He had felt despair before, but this time it was overwhelming.

Father Sheehan felt great sorrow for Michael's suffering. He knew of many young people who, after arriving in America, learned of their parents passing. Perhaps it was best that Michael's parents had found their rest in Cahersiveen. He also knew many of the old folks who came to America only to die of heartbreak, missing their beloved Ireland. The priest offered Michael his deepest sympathy and invited him to kneel with him and pray for their souls.

Michael was grateful for Father Sheehan's friendship. That, along with his newfound devotion to God, helped Michael accept his parents' deaths. Now he looked forward to the arrival next week of his cousin Maria Falvey and his brother Patrick Shea, who were on their way from Cahersiveen to New London. He welcomed seeing family, for at least he wouldn't be so alone in this brutal city.

CHAPTER 16

Emigration of Bridget Murphy Valentia Island, County Kerry, Ireland

May 1880

The two old people sat on the concrete hobs next to the large hearth fireplace, as family and friends gathered for final farewells to Bridget, Julia, and Michael Murphy who were emigrating to America. For the parents, though, it was a day of despair.

The long table beneath the kitchen window held the remains of the fatted pig. Crumbs of brown bread mixed with trails of melted butter ran down the oilcloth, dripping onto the stone floor. Fidgety children sat on the rack (seats) located opposite the hearth. Their bellies full, they were tired from the party and wanted to sleep. A large, shiny wooden dresser stood like a beacon amidst its plainer surroundings, now empty of the few crystal bowls and silver spoons. Bridget reached inside to feel the cool mahogany boards. Among her earliest memories was measuring herself against the shiny brass drawer handles. She'd announce to her mother how much she had grown and insisted that she come to see. When she was little, Bridget couldn't wait to grow up and take her place among the adults in the cottage, and now at the age of fifteen, she wished she were little again, so that she could stay, surrounded by her mother's love.

The traditional Irish farewell "wake" was winding down. Neighbors and family treated the young emigrants with the respect usually reserved for someone lying in a coffin. Relationships between friends, parents, brothers, and sisters became faultless, as they began the process of ceasing to exist to their family in Ireland. Their departure from Valentia was a cause for sadness, and when Bridget and her father faced each other for one last dance, they tried to make it a jig to remember.

The kissing and clasping of hands during the long minutes that remained were uncomfortable to witness, last embraces devastating. During the births of each of their children, Bridget's mother had worn her husband's jacket in the Irish belief that he would bear some of the birthing pain. Whether or not he felt the suffering when the babies were born, now they were both bearing equally the pain of their children's departure.

Bridget turned away from her mother and father, so they couldn't see her tears. She'd heard her mother's mumbled prayers between the sobs. It weakened Bridget's knees, and she didn't know if she had the strength to make it through the door.

A four-wheeled, horse drawn car waited to take them to the train in Killarney. Three Irish draught horses stood tall, heads erect, and ears tense. The mares followed Bridget with their eyes, turning to watch the noisy group accompanying the young people. The driver held tight to the reigns, fearing the commotion would make the horses bolt.

Julia and Michael followed close behind Bridget. The day they dreamed of had finally arrived; they were on their way to America. Yet, now they didn't know if they could make it to the end of the path leading to the main road.

Bridget took one final look at her family's cottage. Her father's old wagon leaned towards the fence next to the turf pile; the slane used to cut the turf was close by. Seed potatoes were covered with a ridge of soil, and she could see the neat rows of drain channels that she and her mother had dug. The potatoes would be ready in August, and it pained her to know she would miss that. Spring shrubs bursting with shades of yellow and pink surrounded her. Bridget bent down to pick some heather and gorse to take with her. At least she'd have a bit of Ireland to remind her of the beautiful wildflowers. She didn't know what to expect when she arrived in America, but she knew everything would be different.

She hoisted her heavy cardboard suitcase onto the car and, gathering up her skirts, boosted herself onto the seat with her back to the cottage and the beloved family who grieved her departure.

Neighbors and family stood with unbroken stillness, watching and waiting for the young emigrants to pass forever out of sight. Slowly, the horse car made its way down the narrow unpaved road, creaking and swaying to the rhythm of the horses' stride. Tears welled up in Bridget's eyes, and she focused them on the gravel. America was so far away, farther than she could ever imagine.

The relentless rain soaked their clothing and parcels. The mares were rotated at changing posts along the way, which gave the young travelers the opportunity to seek shelter in the cottages of kind strangers. Every poor farmer willingly offered a bed to them and a breakfast of oat porridge or, perhaps, an egg and a small slice of bread, for the Irish were generous in the care of each other's children. Bridget removed her boots while in the shelter of a cottage. Her bare feet, calloused and widened by the absence of shoes in her youth, took comfort from the cool, hard-packed earthen floors.

In Killarney, they boarded the train for the port of Queenstown in County Cork. Wide-eyed and anxious, the young Murphy family held tight to their suitcases. Never having ventured even twenty miles past Valentia, they were careful to protect their belongings. The sound of the metal wheels scraping along the train track jolted the passengers, while a great "hiss" of steam drowned out all conversation.

They were absorbed in watching familiar sights—fertile farmlands, quaint little towns, and shimmering lakes surrounded by valleys overflowing with wildflowers.

The overcrowded train swelled with bewildered emigrants. Women busied themselves silencing frightened children, while able-bodied men gathered near the doors to talk of fortunes to be made in America.

The Queenstown pier bustled with feverish activity. Anxious, would-be passengers pushed and shoved their way to get to the front of the line. Bridget, Julia, and Michael stood in line to purchase their tickets. Reaching into her side pocket, Bridget took out the handkerchief that held the money for passage and handed the impatient clerk sixteen pounds and twenty shillings for three third-class tickets. With the tickets safely tucked inside her pocket, Bridget joined the others for the long wait, praying for the protection of Jesus and Mary. Their faith was strong, and the young emigrants remained true to it no matter what.

Bridget secured her suitcase by wrapping her shawl around it. Perspiration collected on her skin, soaked through her wool dress, and ran down her sturdy legs. She wouldn't purchase the water and oatcakes that were being sold by vendors because any money spent in Ireland meant less money for their needs in America.

Convention dictated that emigrants pack one dress or man's suit, woolen petticoat or thick wool jumper (sweater), underclothing, a pair of stockings, handkerchief, hat, brush, two towels, sewing and knitting materials, and a small stock of oatmeal. Suitcases and baskets holding their possessions were checked for any lice that may have found refuge in the hems of their clothing or inside their parcels. Their belongings were sprayed with fumigants, nearly choking them. They suffered through long hours of waiting on the crowded pier. All three of them were checked for typhus, trachoma, and fungus infections.

Small rowboats were being loaded with the weary travelers to take them across the channel to board the Patagonia, the ship they would sail on to America. More than once, Bridget, Julia, and Michael were knocked over in the jostling and bustling and pulled on board like so many bundles.

Before the Patagonia departed, Bridget pushed herself to the front of the crowd for one last look at her beloved homeland. She wondered if she would ever see it again. Some of the passengers could be heard saying that they wouldn't care if they never saw Ireland again, and that they would learn English as well as they could because being Irish was just bad luck.

Because of their innocence and ignorance of the world outside their villages, many emigrants fell victim to charlatans on board the ship. Thievery and brawls occurred all too frequently. The ship's captain provided daily rations of meal, water, and salt, but if weather conditions prevented them from using the deck fires, there would be no rations for the day.

Bridget and her brother and sister waited in long lines to cook their food over the open fires provided for them on deck. If someone had no food, Bridget willingly shared her small amount. The water provided was often foul and muddy and looked as if it had been drawn from a ditch. The rules required the fire to be put out by nightfall. Imagine Bridget's surprise at hearing shouts from overhead and then seeing a bucket of water raining down over a late cook fire. Those who had not yet eaten wouldn't, and if they were in the way, they would be soaked as well. The ten-day journey would prove to be the longest ten days of their lives.

In fine weather, Bridget and her brother Michael stood at the bottom of the ladder and looked through the hatch at the blue sky and white clouds that drifted across the sky.

They all suffered from seasickness. The hold was so thick with the smell of vomit, they could scarcely draw their breath. Whenever there was a bad storm, half the bunks crashed to the floor. Fevers broke out, and the lack of abundant fresh water caused some of the passengers to weaken from thirst. What a torment to be surrounded by so much water, and nothing to drink.

The Patagonia entered the Port of New York on May 15, 1880. Officials from Castle Gardens Boarding Department sent officers to board ships in New York Bay after the boat had passed quarantine inspection. Unsympathetic clerks recorded the number of passengers on board the vessel as well as its state of cleanliness. When the ship docked, a New York City constable and agents from the Landing Department transported the immigrants to the depot via tugboats and barges. They were then marched into Castle Gardens for medical examinations.

The newcomers, sometimes as many as three thousand, were crowded into a rotunda furnished with only wooden benches. The Registering Department, divided into English and foreign language desks, interviewed them and recorded their names, nationalities, country of origin, and destinations. The Forwarding Department mailed letters, remittances, and telegrams for the newly arrived. There was a hospital as well as an insane asylum on the island for those who required treatment for dementia, epilepsy, alcoholism, and mental retardation.

The arrival at Castle Gardens was a harrowing experience. The paperwork, the new surroundings, and the thousands of people bunched together seeking entry into America shocked the siblings. They were amazed at the many different languages spoken by the thousands of immigrants waiting to be processed.

Julia and Michael followed closely behind Bridget, careful to focus on the ground to eliminate any possibility of calling attention to themselves. Exhausted, grimy, and hungry, they wanted nothing to come between them and their final destination—New London, Connecticut.

Waiting in line to be processed, Bridget closed her eyes in order to shut out the ugly sights and sounds of the detention area. Her thoughts wandered to Valentia and her beloved Ballyhearney, to memories of the rolling sea, the deep pinks and purples of the wildflowers, and the fresh air mingled with the aroma from the peat fires. She listened carefully, wishing she could hear the soothing sound of her mother's voice, but instead, the gruff voices of the clerks startled her back to reality.

The officials stamped their arrival cards. Once Bridget, Julia, and Michael were cleared by Immigrations, they proceeded to the money exchange, where they traded their few shillings for U.S. coins to buy food for the one hundred twenty-five mile train ride to New London. They located a small restaurant next to the money exchange where two pounds of rye bread could be purchased for a nickel and bologna was ten cents per pound. Soda water, ginger ale, and sarsaparilla cost five cents. They pooled their few pennies and bought provisions for the journey.

The majority of poor Irish immigrants came to America for factory jobs. No longer trusting their lives to the land because memories of the famines were still fresh, they filled the cities in hopes of learning a trade. The Irish were unpopular immigrants. They brought poverty with them and settled into slums already overpopulated and dangerous. They had endured evictions and famine under English rule and were not easily discouraged by the prejudice they were sure to encounter in Connecticut.

Bridget was surprised by the sounds of an American city. No longer would she awake to the cockcrow or the smell of the oatcakes baking in the hearth. The sound of breaking waves and the smell of the damp fields planted with potatoes were lost to her forever. When she lived in Ireland, she would lie in bed listening to the sounds of her father's heavy boots, the hushed conversations between her parents, and the feather quilts that rustled, signaling the end of sleep, for all of her brothers and sisters shared the same room.

Bridget was unprepared for the sounds of aggressive vendors haggling over prices and noisy wagons pulled by teams of broken-down horses pounding their hooves on the cobblestone streets. The pungent odor of rotted garbage hung thick in the air. Acrid smoke spewed from chimneys; the stench of decaying fish sickened her.

Bridget, Julia, and Michael shared the New London tenement flat with cousins from Valentia Island. Once settled into their cramped quarters, Bridget looked for work. Her servant training at the famed Royal Hotel in Knightstown gave her a certain status. She knew how to polish and protect sterling silver and how to shine wooden floors to a high gloss. Her chapped hands were evidence of the strong lye soaps she had used to scrub sheets and blankets at the British hotel.

Young Bridget searched her sagging pockets for the heather and gorse she had picked on Ballyherney and looked for the small piece of turf tucked inside her suitcase. She held them in her trembling hands as if they were gold. She carefully placed them into her handkerchief and vowed to keep them with her always.

Bridget was determined to become successful. Her arrival in America sparked a fire inside of her. The tattered dress that hung in her cramped closet screamed "Irish immigrant." The first order of business, once she secured employment, was to save enough money for a new dress just like the ones that she had seen in the magazines at the Royal Hotel, a dress that would complement her sapphire blue eyes.

CHAPTER 17

It's Norwich for Bridget Norwich, Connecticut

June 1880-1882

Bridget couldn't believe her good fortune. Just three weeks after arriving in New London, she found herself standing in the grand kitchen of the Taylor family in Norwich, Connecticut.

She noted with delight the odd-shaped pots hanging in neat rows over what appeared to be the cook stove, and she marveled at the sleek coal stove pressed up against the wall, its brass fittings glistening in the spacious sunlit room. An assortment of muffins and cakes lay cooling on the grates atop the cook stove. Steam rolled from a large kettle, and the succulent aroma of roast beef permeated the air. She was amazed at the efficiency of the stove, for there were pies in the warming closet, bread baking in the oven, meat simmering in the tin roaster while tea simmered on the top burner. She couldn't wait to tell her brother and sister about the marvels of cooking in a kitchen fit for a king.

Delicate china plates of all shapes and sizes were displayed on crowded shelves attached to the massive plastered walls. Gas lamps flickered and brightened the room as the sun moved away from the diamond paned windows, signaling the servants to begin preparations for the meal. Bridget donned her apron and commenced scooping mashed potatoes from a large earthenware pot, using the metal spoon that hung alongside the stove.

She followed the other servants into the dining room. Hot biscuits were stacked at each end of the table, assorted vegetables surrounded large platters of meat and potatoes, and delicious desserts crowded the linen-covered table. Bridget had never seen such a variety of food, and each dish looked more delicious than the next. Any remaining food would be dinner for the servants, so it seemed fitting to always add a little extra meat and potatoes to the pot.

Bridget described the grand home to her family as being a high house, so tall it stretched up towards the sky. Thick, lush carpets covered the rich wood floors, and custom-made mahogany furniture polished to a high gloss glistened in the parlor. Richly embroidered overstuffed couches wrapped themselves in front of marble fireplaces. The mistress insisted Bridget dust each day, as the coal residue created a constant stream of grimy dust that settled on the furniture.

The Taylor family preferred Irish girls for servants because they possessed high standards of morality and honesty. They also knew the Irish suffered economic hardship, thus delaying any marriage plans.

Bridget admired the clock that stood tall on the mantle. In Ireland the full-throated cockcrow guaranteed an early rising, and she knew the time of day by looking at the posi-

tion of the sun. She couldn't wait to write to her family in
Ireland telling them of the beautiful home she worked
in—a house with more than three rooms and meat on the
table every night.

Bridget accepted the position in Norwich because it
paid the most, and even though it was ten miles from her
family in New London, she knew that she could see them
on holidays. If Bridget were not to see all of her siblings or
cousins for a time, at least she would have the company of
the two Irish girls she worked with.

Pleased to have a bedroom to herself, she unpacked
each of her personal items and placed them carefully
inside the sturdy dresser drawer. She removed the dried
heather and gorse from the rolled handkerchief that she
had brought with her from Ballyhearney and placed them
in a secure spot. She was lonely for her mother's touch and
missed the family she left behind. Bridget sat on the corner of her bed, ashamed to seem so ungrateful for God's
goodness. She clutched her rosary beads and began to pray
for strength to accept God's will. The small piece of turf
that she carried from Ireland peeked out from underneath
her tattered handkerchief. The little bit of Ireland that she
carried with her from Ballyhearney meant more to her
than anything.

Bridget's days were busy. The demands of cooking,
cleaning, laundry, and minding the two young children
kept her in motion all day and well into the evening.
Rising early, she filled the belly of the stove with kindling
and coal to warm the kitchen while she prepared breakfast.
She filled the pots with meat and vegetables and put them
on the stove to simmer for the evening meal. She brushed

the carpets and aired the bed linens. On Friday nights, she boiled numerous pots of water for the children's baths, after which she tucked each of them into bed. Then the mister and mistress required attention. Their baths were drawn and their beds turned down, and steamy hot water bottles were placed at their feet. After all of that, she gathered the discarded clothing, making sure to scrub them clean before retiring for the evening.

Each week, 292 pounds of coal was hauled into the kitchen, along with fourteen pounds of kindling to help ignite the fire. Twenty-seven pounds of ash had to be shoveled out of the stove each week and deposited in buckets that were then dumped into the garden. Each night, Bridget fell exhausted into bed. Although grateful for her blessings, she often wondered if she would ever live a life without the burden of being a servant.

Bridget made herself at home in the parish church down the street. She loved the grandeur of St. Patrick's. Its gothic spires thrust upwards towards the sky, and the heavy wooden doors required the strength of the saints to open. She derived great pleasure from helping Father Shatran set up for Sunday morning Mass and even sewed some of the vestments for the high holy days. She found comfort spending time in the church, where she enjoyed the company of parishioners, sharing lively conversations.

On Sunday mornings Bridget and the other servant girls could be seen going to church dressed in rich satin dresses, elegant bonnets, parasols, and gloves that were hand-me-downs from their employers. Lovely gaiter boots were buttoned up the side and polished to a high gloss. These girls, who grew up in floorless mud cabins covered with thatch and went to church without shoes or stockings, now enjoyed their unaccustomed luxuries.

Domestic service provided a glimpse of middle-class America, and exposed Bridget to the modern world. In a very real sense, this American home was her school, where she received an education in the social lives of well-to-do women.

Mr. Taylor voiced his concern over the servants' devotion to the Catholic Church. There was talk around the neighborhood that some of the Irish girls might be agents of the Pope, bent on converting the Protestant children in their charge. Priding themselves on their British ancestry and their Protestant faith, the Taylors believed the Irish traits of ignorance and superstition were attributed to the influence of Catholicism. Bridget was ordered to conceal her rosary from the children, and she was forbidden to tell them bedtime stories. She was instructed to read from the King James Bible and to accompany the children to Protestant services each Sunday morning.

Bridget accepted the mandate only because she felt she had no choice. She had worked for the Taylor family for two years, and they paid her well. Her meals and room were far above what the other servant girls in the area had, and with the influx of Europeans, jobs this good were scarce.

She managed to escort the children to their church after hurrying back from the Mass at St. Patrick's. Suffering through the Protestant service, Bridget recalled stories her mother told of how she had survived the religious prejudice that plagued Ireland. They concealed the Catholic priest in their hut in the years before the famine, so he could offer Mass to the few people brave enough to risk eviction if they were caught. She remembered stories of how Catholic priests hid in ditches and how her family concealed the chalice and vestments used in celebration of the Mass. Catholicism was outlawed in Ireland, and any priest or parishioner found celebrating the Mass suffered tremendously at the hands of the English.

Feelings of helplessness crept into Bridget's heart and, as good as life was in America, she felt sad that the twin devil's of hatred and prejudice had followed her across the sea. This new development caused her to re-think her life as a servant, and she began to turn her thoughts to becoming independent. After all, she hadn't devoted herself to the Taylor family for the last two years for the privilege of being told where to pray.

Bridget used the St. Patrick's confessional as the place to vent her anger. She knew it was a sin to harbor resentment, and she prayed for strength. Father Shatran understood her anguish. He also knew that the majority of the people in town were anti-Catholic, but more especially, they were anti-Irish. The priest felt this isolation only added to their difficult work situations.

Father Shatran contacted the parish priest in New London to enlist his help in creating a social gathering on Saturday nights at St. Patrick's Church. Father Sheehan from St. Mary, Star of the Sea Church in New London was happy to assist. Together, they set out to arrange a party for their marriageable parishioners. Announcements were posted at each of the churches, and all the young Irish singles were invited.

An evening of dance and merriment! Oh, wouldn't that be something. Bridget hadn't thought about the music of the fiddles and the pipes for a long time. She conveyed her enthusiasm to the two other Irish girls, and they agreed to go to the dance with her. All week they hummed the old songs while they worked, and sometimes found themselves giggling like schoolgirls.

CHAPTER 18

Michael and Bridget Meet

November 1882

The parish hall resounded with soul-awakening music that echoed throughout the church. The Saturday evening penitents were only slightly bothered by the revelers. It was good to hear the Irish music blended with the erratic shuffling of the boots of the young people in the parish hall. The virtuous old women, gathered for prayer, recalled their own vigorous youth when they danced the Irish jig in their country towns.

Father Shatran heard about Michael from Father Sheehan and was thrilled to have found an expert dancer to help lead the Saturday evening dances. Because of Michael, the weekly dances were popular among the Irish young people in the New London/Norwich area. And the priest was impressed by his quiet, reserved manner.

Bridget stirred the fruit punch while her friends arranged trays of ripe cheese and sliced bread. Flickering gas lamps threw shadows across the room that reflected off the mirrors. The wooden floors gleamed, each board polished to perfection. The long table held buttery, rich desserts baked by the women of the parish. Freshly laundered linens and faceted crystal punch bowls graced the table. It promised to be a wonderful evening, and Bridget smiled at the thought of dancing.

Michael dabbed at his forehead. His handkerchief embarrassed him, so he was careful to keep the tattered edges hidden in the palm of his hand. He knew he looked particularly handsome, dressed in his new suit and shiny leather boots, and he didn't want the handkerchief to detract from his appearance. He had taken care to shave closer than usual and slick back his hair; a loose wave dipped across his forehead. He recalled the dances at the crossroads in Cahersiveen, but they couldn't compare with this wonderful night in the parish hall in Norwich. Joyous laughter and the happy conversations of the young people helped ease the pangs of homesickness for many of the Irish who, like Michael, were lonely.

Father Sheehan stood at the entrance to welcome the young people in from the frosty night. Simple yet elegant coats hung against the wall, creating a colorful patchwork pattern of deep gold and rich burgundies. It was a wonderful evening, a magical evening!

The young woman standing at the punch bowl caught Michael's eye. Her thick lashes cast shadows on her soft cheeks, and her emerald green satin dress hung in folds from her shoulders and was cinched at her waist. Dozens of rhinestone buttons sparkled, reflecting the light of the tall candles that had been placed on the table.

Michael approached Bridget cautiously. He noticed how gracefully her hands moved, expertly placing the ladle over each tiny crystal goblet, careful not to waste a drop. Bridget didn't notice Michael staring at her, for had she seen him, she surely would have laughed. He stood there gawking, and for all his fine suit, close shave, and slicked-back hair, he looked like a schoolboy.

Bridget swayed to the music and tapped her foot, keeping perfect time with the fiddle. She looked up just in time to catch Michael's beaming smile. Returning the smile, she put down the ladle and moved away from the table. She joined her friends who were engaged in conversation with the young men who had recently arrived. One of them noticed Bridget and asked her to dance.

Bridget and her partner joined in the two lines separating the men from the women. When the music began, Bridget stepped towards her partner. When the tempo increased, they placed their hands on their hips and performed a variety of lively movements. They twirled, stepped, and laughed out loud.

Father Shatran watched from across the room. He saw the disappointment on Michael's face. The priest smiled, thinking how nice if the two of them could meet. He knew Bridget as a gracious young woman, highly regarded among her friends, and respected within the parish. She radiated an inner beauty and lit up the room with her smile and her charming personality.

Even though Michael was busy teaching the dance, he couldn't erase Bridget from his thoughts. He had never seen such beauty in all of County Kerry, and he wondered what part of Ireland she was from. He lost sight of Bridget in the noisy crowd. Searching the throng of dancers, he spied her at the entrance talking to Father Sheehan. He looked away for only a moment, and when he looked back, she was gone. Disappointed, he hurried to Father Sheehan's side to ask about the dark-haired beauty in the emerald green dress.

Father Sheehan had never seen Michael so animated. Careful not to embarrass him, he pretended not to notice the interest Michael showed in the lovely young lady.

Michael danced with many of the girls during the evening but never once looked into their eyes, for it was Bridget's eyes that had captured his soul. Oh, but she was a looker, he thought, as he tried hard to concentrate on the dance.

On Sunday after Mass, Bridget hurried to the Taylor home. She had promised Mrs. Taylor she would arrive in time to accompany the girls to their Protestant service. Last week she was late because she stopped to talk to the priest and had lost all track of time. This week, Mrs. Taylor reminded her to be on time. She ran down the street, her cape flying out behind her.

The holidays were approaching. That meant she would have little time for herself. The girls needed new dresses, and Bridget would be busy every night for the next couple of months, sewing and helping prepare the mansion for the Christmas parties.

Meanwhile, Michael continued to look for the pretty girl who wore the green dress, but she hadn't attended the dances in weeks. Thoughts of her consumed him; he worried he might never see her again. He continued to teach the dance and enjoyed his role as the dance master, but he couldn't shake from his mind the vision of the pretty young lady he saw that Saturday night in November.

Bridget turned eighteen on January 15, 1883. That was a Saturday, and she and her friends thought it would be nice to celebrate the event at the parish church dance. Bridget had a gold dress embroidered with tiny maroon colored roses. She had sewed it herself and had been saving it for a special occasion. Tonight, dancing the Irish jig, she would show off her beautiful new dress.

As soon as she made her way into the parish hall, she noticed the tall, handsome young man who had smiled at her that night in November. He was dancing with a pretty red-haired girl.

As his partner danced around him, Michael's eyes suddenly locked with Bridget's. He didn't remember ending the dance because he never heard the music stop. Michael saw the other young men admiring her; he was sure they all noticed the soft gold color of the dress and her radiant beauty. Michael promised himself he would meet her before the end of the evening.

Bridget's brother, her sister, and her cousins Nora and Nellie Murphy had surprised her by showing up at the dance. She was delighted to have their company, and they fussed over her while toasting her birthday. Michael heard Bridget's laughter from across the room.

It was now or never, he said to himself. Pasting a look of confidence on his face—but fearing his knees would weaken the minute she spoke to him—he approached Bridget and asked her to dance. As if in a dream, he guided her through the routine of the jig. Looking into her brilliant blue eyes, he thought he would die from the pleasure of it. When the music stopped, he introduced himself. Bridget asked what part of Ireland he was from and hearing the name of Cahersiveen made her smile. She told him that they had been neighbors in Ireland—and now in Connecticut, as well.

They spent the evening dancing and talking with friends and family. Everybody who learned it was her birthday sang to her in celebration. She couldn't remember ever having such a good time since arriving in America. Bridget was happy she met Michael, and Michael couldn't believe his good fortune.

Father Sheehan and Father Shatran stood in the corner by the narrow entrance. As they watched Michael and Bridget, they knew their Sunday prayers would include special blessings for two of their favorite parishioners.

CHAPTER 19

'Tis a Blessed Day

February 1885

Michael's job demanded strength. He worked every muscle shoveling tons of cement into three-wheeled carts. His body ached. The sheer bulk of the iron bull tongue made his arms tingle with pain. Quarry work in Ireland was backbreaking, but digging roads and pouring concrete in Connecticut was worse. The humid, sun-drenched summer days, and the freezing temperatures of the winter months taxed his resolve.

After work, Michael trudged to the rooming house in time to join his family for a serving of good boiled meat and fresh vegetables. His cousin Maria prepared excellent meals for him and his brother Patrick. She baked their favorite breads and worked miracles with inferior pieces of meat purchased from the butcher. She used her feminine charms and keen wit to wrangle fresh cabbages, potatoes, and turnips from the neighborhood grocer. Maria watched the poor Irish girls leave his shop with food fit for the garbage, and she had no intention of accepting anything less than fresh food.

Father Sheehan helped them locate decent living quarters. They now had a little extra space in which to live more comfortably. Maria learned how to use the kitchen stove, and Patrick made sure there was always enough coal for the fire. Michael enjoyed the company of family but couldn't seem to get Bridget out of his thoughts. The priest encouraged him to find a good woman to marry; he knew Michael needed a wife to care for him.

Bridget liked her independence. She felt she was too young to be serious about anyone, yet she continued to attend the Saturday night dances at St. Patrick's and enjoy Michael's company. She wrote to her family in Ireland, telling them how fortunate she was to have met a man from Cahersiveen. It surprised Michael and Bridget to learn that they knew the same families. They talked about the dances at the Crossroads and the fairs on Main Street when the farmers brought their livestock to Cahersiveen to sell for the best prices, and they laughed remembering the Valentia farmers loading cows onto rowboats to take across the channel. Sometimes they were silent, thinking their own thoughts of home.

There was talk about Michael and Bridget getting married. The two young people seemed to get along well, and everyone thought them perfectly matched. But, Bridget had become accustomed to earning money. For the first time in her life, she was able to afford beautiful dresses and stylish hats, and she didn't want to be too quick to give those luxuries up. Besides, her family in Ireland had become accustomed to her remittances, and they relied on her generosity. Father Sheehan took every opportunity to talk with Bridget about Michael's wonderful qualities. She could tell the priest admired and respected Michael for his kind heart and generous spirit; that influenced her decision.

Michael and Bridget found themselves planning a wedding—their wedding. Family and friends busied themselves with the preparations, leaving the young couple to plan their lives together. The wedding was set for February 17, 1885 in the church of St. Patrick's in Norwich, Connecticut, with the Reverend Shatran officiating. Father Sheehan from St. Mary's offered to assist in the ceremony. A reception would be held in the church hall where the couple first met and danced.

It was a grand affair! Bridget sewed her wedding dress from various scraps of material that she had saved. Small beaded pearls were sewn to the bodice by hand, and numerous tiny buttons pulled the dress tight in the back. Bridget's sister fussed with the bride's hair and attached the long white veil. She knew Bridget worried about how they would ever be able to afford the children that God would send them, but she also knew her sister loved Michael, and that would make all things right.

Patrick made sure his brother's white shirt was laundered stiff at the collar and cuffs and his shoes were repaired and shined for the glorious event. He knew Michael was nervous—marriage was a huge step in a man's life, for it wasn't every day you accepted the responsibilities of a wife in these uncertain times. Michael had many discussions with Father Sheehan and asked for the priest's blessing on this very special day.

Michael stood before the altar next to his bride. Bridget was a vision of loveliness, and Michael wished his mother could see the beautiful Irish lady that was his new wife.

Many family members and friends attended. Bridget's employer supplied a fabulous meal to celebrate the special occasion. Silver serving dishes, crystal glasses, and china plates were carried into the church hall from the Taylor dining room and set on the long tables. Irish music played, and people ate, drank, and danced all evening. Michael and Bridget danced the jig until the wee hours of the morning. Everyone toasted the happy couple. Father Shatran and Father Sheehan prayed they be blessed with many children.

It was the next month that Bridget found herself pregnant. Their first child was due in November. Bridget had moved in with Michael and his cousin Maria and brother Patrick. It was crowded, but they enjoyed each other's company and so, for a short time, the arrangement worked just fine. And Bridget now lived closer to her family in New London. She enjoyed the days spent with her brother, sister, and cousins, and for a time, life seemed good.

Michael's wages paid the rent with enough left over for food. Bridget had quit her job when she married Michael, as was the custom. Michael's cousin Maria was planning to get married to an Irish fellow she met at her factory job, and Patrick worked on the fishing boats. Michael was happy to see his family getting along so well in America.

On November 23, 1885, John Michael Shea was born in the bedroom his parents shared with Maria and Patrick. Baby John was guided into the world by the expert hands of a mid-wife. Michael beamed when he heard the cries of his new son.

Bridget and Michael adored their baby boy and happily settled into their role as parents. They carried him to church every Sunday to show him off and always lingered after Mass to chat with Father Sheehan.

A year later, Bridget was pregnant with their second child. She worried how they would manage, because Michael had lost his job and was having difficulty finding another one. The new wave of European immigrants, able to read and write, were snatching the good-paying jobs from the Irish. Michael found himself working harder and earning less than when he had first arrived in New London. He accepted temporary work on the docks, but that was only seasonal and paid a paltry wage.

Their families helped the young couple prepare for the new baby. They fussed over Bridget and told Michael that God would provide. They would just have to keep the faith.

On July 6, 1887, James Patrick Shea entered the world. Michael beamed because he was now the proud father of two beautiful little boys. For a moment he put his worries aside and basked in the pleasure of his family.

Bridget kept busy cooking, cleaning, and caring for the two small children. The living quarters were cramped, and Bridget knew they would soon have to look for a place of their own. But she also knew this couldn't happen until Michael secured permanent, good-paying work.

Michael continued to work as a day laborer. His strength gave him the advantage over the older men, but the work was only temporary, and he worried about the future of his wife and sons.

Many months later, Bridget found herself pregnant with their third child. Michael continued to struggle to feed his growing family, wondering how they were going to build the life he had dreamed of in New London. He began to think that would not be possible as long as he stayed in Connecticut.

His friends told him about the meatpacking houses that were opening in Omaha, Nebraska. They spoke of agents who were signing up anyone willing to go west and settle in the Central Plains. The work was difficult and dangerous, but the wages were good. Curious, he walked down to the train station to hear for himself what Omaha had to offer.

Bridget's pregnancy went well, and little Daniel was welcomed into the world on a snowy December day in 1890. He was smaller than their other two boys. Father Sheehan had transferred to a parish in one of the southern states, leaving Father O'Connell to officiate the baptism. Father O'Connell suggested they baptize Daniel on his day of birth because he worried about the little one.

Bridget listened carefully as her husband explained why they had to leave New London and move to Omaha, Nebraska. But she didn't know how she could be separated from her family. Leaving Ireland was enough to kill the spirit, and now she was asked to travel with her babies to the God-forsaken place called Nebraska.

Bridget prayed for the strength to accept this burden while she cried to Father O'Connell. He ached for the young Shea family; their life was difficult enough being immigrants, and being Irish meant even more hardship. He had seen many young people rise in the ranks of New London society, but he could see that Michael and Bridget would be struggling a long time to afford even the bare necessities. If they must leave, then that would be the will of God. They prayed, and afterwards, Bridget went to tell Michael she would be ready to travel within the week.

CHAPTER 20

Welcome to Porkopolis South Omaha, Nebraska

August 1891

Bridget peered out the murky window of the train at the passing landscape, while the conductor traced lines on a map to show her sons their route. The names of the states—Pennsylvania, Ohio, Indiana, Illinois, and Iowa—sounded so strange. She never heard such words, and she doubted her children knew why they were making the trip. Nevertheless, she appreciated the conductor's kindness and knew the boys were already homesick for New London. She replayed the farewell scene in her mind: the hugs, the crying, and the final wave good-bye. She swore to Michael that if she ever had to say good-bye to family again, it would be her death.

The swaying of the steam locomotive rocked the children to sleep. They had asked so many questions. Would their aunts and uncles be in Omaha? Would they have beds of their own, a park to play in, and a long wooden pier to watch the ships from? In New London, Bridget knew all the right words to comfort them. But now, she hesitated to tell them anything. She couldn't because she didn't know herself what to expect.

She looked at Michael, whose profile remained steady, despite the sidling movement of the train. His rough, calloused hands rested on his threadbare trousers. He was wearing the same suit that he had worn when they first met at the St. Patrick's dance. She smiled, recalling how it had taken two years for him to persuade her to become his wife. It would be an Irishman she'd be marrying and she did well to find a man from Cahersiveen. There was an infinite goodness and comfortable warmth about the man who now was so alone with his thoughts.

Carefully inspecting each fingernail, Michael continued to worry about the decision to move his young family to the wild plains of Nebraska. Just six years ago, cowboys, gunfights, and saloons were as much a part of the town as horses and herds of cattle galloping up the dirt streets. The agent for the slaughterhouses, whose job it was to persuade men to move their families to South Omaha, said there had been five women in the town only five years ago. Michael didn't tell Bridget everything because he knew she would disapprove. Nevertheless, he had no choice but to move his family to Omaha. They had lived too long in poverty and on handouts. Michael knew that they might never see any of their families again. Bridget had cried for days. He caused her much pain and because of that, he felt dispirited.

Michael reached for Bridget's hand, the one that comforted baby Daniel. The child slept fitfully, and both he and Bridget worried about him. Their two older sons were hardy, growing strong and straight, but Daniel ate little and slept most of the time. Glancing at his wife, Michael read the concern on her face as she tucked the soft flannel blanket around the restless child.

Thinking back to the evening at St. Patrick's Church six years ago, he recalled the passionate feelings that had stirred in him when he saw Bridget. A lovely Irish girl, she carried her heritage like royalty. Michael knew that he was going to marry her; it was just a question of when she would have him.

The journey from Connecticut to Nebraska took approximately three days on the Transcontinental Railway. Meals of warm milk and oats had to satisfy the children's hunger. Sandwiches and tea could be purchased for less than twenty cents from vendors who came onto the train.

John and James were fascinated by their surroundings. The beds that hung from the walls captured the boys' imagination. They pretended to be conductors and distributed pieces of scrap paper at each stop. The porter laughed at the boys' antics and was glad to provide them with an activity, so that their mother could focus attention on her bundled child.

The passengers cheered when they left the flat plains of Iowa to cross the Missouri River. The city of Omaha seemed to spring up from the fields as the locomotive chugged laboriously to the train station in the center of town. Passengers leaned from the windows for their first glimpse of the "Magic City." Four major meatpacking plants in South Omaha were the backbone of Omaha's economy.

The train hissed and jerked to a halt. Bridget and Michael gathered their few belongings, straightened their sons' wrinkled clothing, and got off the train. Waiting in line with so many others, Bridget was reminded of her arrival at Castle Gardens eleven years earlier. She recalled how young and enthusiastic she was then. Now, at the seasoned age of twenty-six with a husband and three small children, she felt apprehensive about living in a "cowboy town."

John and James reacted to the disgusting smell of the foul air by coughing into their shirts and pretending to gag. The stench hung so thick in the air they could almost see it. The boys pointed to large smoke stacks belching out fumes from the distant stockyards. Bridget buried her face in her sleeve. "You'll get used to the smell," the agent told them. "It'll be in your clothes, drift in your windows, and be there at every meal. Yep! You'll sure get used to it," the agent said, as he tipped his hat. He repeated this speech many times while he greeted the new employees and their families. People always reacted the same way when they smelled Omaha.

When Michael's name was called, his weary family pushed through the noisy crowd. The agent handed Michael a tag identifying him as a new employee of Swift & Company, where he would slaughter hogs and cattle for market. Though the work would be unpleasant, Michael knew he could perform the task easily, for he had helped his mother slaughter the pigs and hang them to smoke in the hearth.

The agent ushered the families to the open carriages and then handed the driver directions to the tenements in South Omaha. The bags were tossed onto the floor, and each of the passengers was hoisted onto the bench seats.

John and James sat up front with the driver, watching him as he jockeyed the mares through the filthy streets. The horses kicked up enough mud to muck up the floor of the carriage. Its benches, soiled with mud and horse manure, sagged under the weight of its passengers.

Bridget focused on her sons' laughter. Their youth and innocence provided a constant source of pleasure for her.

It pleased her to see the "skyscrapers" of downtown Omaha—the New York Life Insurance Company, the large Opera House, the busy Omaha Bee Newspaper, and the new school building. She wished her boys to have every advantage, and Omaha looked as though it could provide the education and sophistication important to her.

With 8,000 residents, South Omaha was the fastest growing city in the nation. Vast quantities of chops, bacon, and steaks were shipped from the slaughterhouses every day. But Omaha and South Omaha were as different as night and day; the only characteristic they shared was the stench of the stockyards. Bridget was disappointed to see that South Omaha had only blacksmith shops, shabby boarding houses, churches without spires, and a lot of saloons. The first-deputy of South Omaha was a former policeman, and his principal job was keeping intoxicated drovers from tearing up the town.

The carriage pulled up to a ramshackle two-story wooden building, one of several barracks that were balanced on concrete piers to keep them from sinking into the earth. Bridget had expected better but said nothing as she gathered up their few belongings.

Michael enjoyed conversations with the men who would be their neighbors. Some of them had come from

Boston, others from Ohio and Pennsylvania, but all of them had come for work. The majority were immigrants from Ireland, and talk of their homeland dominated the lively conversation.

The Shea family settled into their new home, a shack with two narrow beds jammed into a small back room. A rusty water pump looked as though it hadn't been used in years, and a dirty kitchen sink hung from a cracked plaster wall. Skimpy curtains provided a small amount of privacy. Bridget went about making the place as comfortable as possible. She hung their patched and wrinkled clothing on a rope pulled tight from one end of the kitchen to the other. The stove was adequate, and Bridget was thankful for the icebox that stood next to the door. At least she could keep the milk cool and had a place to store meat and vegetables.

August in Nebraska was a scorcher. Bridget thought she would suffocate from the heat and humidity. Grime and soot stuck to their clothing and settled onto their food. They couldn't afford the extra fifteen cents for another fifty-pound block of ice to keep their perishables cool because Bridget's budget covered only three ice deliveries per week.

The boys, oblivious to the heat and discomfort, ran barefoot through the town, played stickball with their friends, and helped Bridget carry supplies home from the market. They wished they could afford a horse carriage like the ones they saw parked in front of Semins Grocery at 36th and T Street, but they knew better than to think that could happen. Bridget sent them to the Cudahy and Armour Packing Plants to purchase meat; it was cheaper there than at the grocer's. It seemed to take them forever to make that trip, so when soup meat went on sale for ten cents, Bridget allowed them to spend two cents on licorice sticks to tide them over on their journey home.

Bridget and Michael were members of the St. Agnes Parish on Q Street. Reverend Moriarty served his parishioners well and dedicated himself to helping each family. Bridget and Michael took a strong liking to the young priest and often invited him for Sunday dinners.

Michael's steady income allowed the family to put aside a bit of his five-dollar per week salary so that one day they could afford to buy a home of their own. Because his weekly salary barely covered rent, food, clothing, and other necessities for the growing family, Michael worked extra shifts in order to build their "home fund."

They were a good Irish Catholic family who centered their lives on their children. The neighbor women envied Bridget. Her husband never staggered home from saloons at night. The drinking curse of the Irish found no home with Michael.

1892

In October, Bridget found herself pregnant with their fourth child, due to arrive in June. She wrote letters to her family in Ireland telling of their three beautiful sons and their "adventurous" lives in South Omaha. Her letters went unanswered, but she continued to write in hope that one day she would receive a reply.

Frequently, while scrubbing the laundry and hanging it out, Bridget's thoughts drifted to Ireland. She missed the fresh sea air of Valentia and her large family. The pieces of heather and gorse she had carried to America remained her most treasured possession. While telling her boys stories of Ireland, she found herself choking back tears. She lived every day with a pain in her heart, for she missed her beloved Ballyhearney. Her sisters in New London wrote to her of their hard times. She wished they would join her in South Omaha, but they preferred to live where the Atlantic Ocean could be heard rushing to the shore.

Michael carried home the remnants of slaughtered animals on his blood-splattered boots. Grease-like stains tattooed his clothing, and his hands bore the scars from the butcher knives used to cut the throats of the reluctant hogs. Bridget scrubbed her floors and Michael's clothes until her knuckles bled, but there was no way the smell and stain of the stockyards could be erased.

Nothing prepared them for the freezing weather that settled into Omaha that winter. The biting winds drove the temperatures below the zero mark; snow drifted beneath their front door and made its way through the cracks in the windows. The coal stove had no rest from the relentless six-month run of harsh weather.

The advent of spring brought warm breezes along with the ever-present mud of the soggy ground. The boys kicked off their boots and ran through the town, comfortable at last in their bare feet. Bridget made herself at home in Nebraska for the sake of her family, but she feared for her sanity. She wondered if she could survive another winter as horrible as the one that just passed.

The new baby arrived on June 30th. Thomas Edward was ushered into the world by a mid-wife. The Shea family had grown to four sons and had outgrown the tiny tenement. Michael knew they would soon need a home of their own.

Outbreaks of diphtheria, smallpox, and cholera ran rampant throughout the town, finding their way into the tenement that housed the Shea family. Bridget stayed up nights with twenty-month old Daniel. His body raged with fever, and he became too weak to hold up his head. The doctor told them to keep him warm and to make sure he drank lots of fluids. Michael hauled coal from the yard. As hot as it was outside, they had to heat the tenement until the kitchen was like an oven. The family fanned themselves while keeping Daniel close to the stove. Bridget feared any draft would make the little one weaker. Meanwhile, she continued to care for her other three sons, keeping them separated from Daniel, who might be contagious.

With each passing hour, Bridget could feel Daniel slipping away. He became delirious and refused to eat or drink. They prayed to the saints and to Jesus and Mary to make their little boy well and strong, but it was not to be. Little Daniel died in Bridget's arms on the evening of August 14th. Father Moriarty stayed the night to pray the rosary, and neighbors came to prepare the body for burial. Bridget thought she would go out of her mind with grief. Michael held her but could do little to comfort her. The small wooden box was carried into the cemetery of St. Mary's on Q Street, and Daniel was laid to rest beside a young oak tree.

They continued their lives, although not with the same energy. Bridget went through the motions of caring for her three surviving children and grieving husband. There was no consoling them. Father Moriarty continued to pray for the family. He admired and respected them for their unwavering faith.

Two months after Daniel's death on October 27th, Michael filed his Intent to become a United States Citizen. He could barely sign his name to the document that stated he "renounced forever his allegiance to The Queen of Great Britain and Ireland, of whom he was a subject." Michael's talents didn't include an ability to read or write with the degree of accuracy required to pass the written test. It was his fondest wish for himself and Bridget to become citizens, but it couldn't happen yet. Bridget secretly wished that the law allowed her to make application because she was able to read and write, but women were not recognized as citizens with authority and strong opposition to women's suffrage continued.

1893-94

In 1893, a financial depression hit the country. Michael and Bridget had to suffer yet another devastating setback. The Nebraska Savings Bank failed, and the Shea family savings were lost, their home fund gone.

May 1894 brought a scorching drought. Temperatures reached 105 degrees in the month of May. Then a late frost on May 17th caused severe crop damage throughout the county. Corn had to be replanted, and the wheat and oat crops were nearly destroyed. Summer brought temperatures of 112 degrees. Fresh vegetables were scarce, and Bridget's small garden withered with the drought. The children all suffered from croup, and Bridget received precious little sleep while caring for them.

On September 4, 1894, Bridget gave birth to another son, Michael, Jr. She was sure that Daniel's spirit had been reborn in the new baby, and that thought lifted her spirits.

Michael, Jr. was a fussy baby. He caught cold easily, and his labored breathing frightened Bridget. She offered him small amounts of sugar water between feedings to fill him. She rocked him for hours in front of the coal stove and prayed to all the saints in heaven for his recovery. He began to respond to his mother's care. His cough quieted and his brow cooled. Bridget was sure her baby had miraculously recovered.

But when she went to wake him in the morning, his body was cold and still. Not wanting to believe what she knew to be true, she held him gently and spoke in the Irish. She cried until she had no more tears to spill. Baby Michael died from pneumonia on December 15th. He joined his brother Daniel under the young oak tree in St. Mary's Cemetery.

The spirit of the holiday did not visit the Shea home that Christmas or on any holidays that followed. Bridget and Michael mourned the loss of another child with as much dignity as they could muster, but their hearts ached with silent anguish and pain. Father Moriarty visited each day to pray with them, and with those prayers came the strength to help them cope with their losses.

1896-98

In July Bridget was irritable and complained of backaches. She blamed the unrelenting heat for her short temper and was surprised when she learned she was pregnant. She knew the time had come to leave the tenement. They had scrimped and saved in order to escape their appalling surroundings. Bridget also needed to move away from the old Irish biddies with their talk of the fairies stealing the souls of her babies from their cradles.

On September 16, 1896, Michael and Bridget purchased their home at 3715 U Street in South Omaha. They paid one thousand dollars to Mary J. C. Ryan to secure the Warrantee Deed. The new development was situated on the subdivided farm property of the Corrigan family. This area of South Omaha, nicknamed "The Hill," was home to many Irish immigrants.

The house was situated on a deeply rutted dirt road that stopped just short of a ragged picket fence. Michael assured Bridget that a good coat of paint, along with a few minor repairs, was all that was needed to dress it up. Walnut wood floors creaked and groaned under the weight of their boots. A wide border of thick, polished molding ran the length and width of the room. The walls were painted a dark shade of blue. Three small glass shades extended from the gas pipe that hung from the ceiling. Daylight streaming through the narrow front window illuminated their way into the small dining room. Identical to the living room in size and color, Bridget could easily imagine serving meals under the soft glow of the gas lamp. A narrow staircase led up to an attic/bedroom as well as down to the cellar. Peering into the tiny kitchen, she saw the water pump set on the dry sink with a medium size wooden bucket beneath the spigot to catch the precious drips. A wooden icebox stood across the room from the small coal stove. The dark linoleum on the floor curled at the corners and showed much wear by the back door.

Bridget and Michael's bedroom was next to the living room. It was papered in a large floral print. Gas lamps hung from the walls, and the front window provided an unobstructed view of the cheerless U Street. The yard was large enough for Bridget's garden, and there was an ample side area for a chicken coop. A rickety wooden outhouse leaned towards the alley. Michael's first duty would be to straighten and secure it.

In Bridget's eyes, the house was a castle. They finally had a place to call their own! Bridget shed tears of happiness, and Michael felt proud to be a homeowner in the grand city of South Omaha. They wasted no time moving their meager belongings into their new home for fear that, if they hesitated, it would all disappear.

Bridget knew she was pregnant when they bought the house, but waited to tell Michael the good news. As expected, Michael was overjoyed by the announcement.

On March 19, 1897, Francis Joseph joined the family on U Street, another boy for Michael and Bridget.

James, John, and Thomas shared the upstairs bedroom of the little bungalow. Baby Francis remained close to Bridget. She needed to protect him from the curse that seemed to have fallen on them. She guarded the newborn—her unceasing vigilance noted by everyone. Her sons grew strong and handsome under her watchful eye and, much to his parents delight, Francis was also a robust child.

Omaha needed a boost to show that the West had recovered from the financial panic of 1893. Temporary structures made of horsehair and plaster of Paris were constructed to house the Trans Mississippi International Exposition's five-month run. Dignitaries came from all over the world to view the exhibits. They featured the flushing toilet, faucets, X-ray machines, incandescent light bulbs, and the incubator for pre-mature infants. Michael, Bridget, and their children examined the new electrically operated appliances, motors, and equipment of the future and were stunned by the magic of the lights that adorned the Grand Court buildings at night. They tasted Jell-O, sno-cones, and Boston baked beans for the first time. Omaha was humming, and the Shea family eagerly participated in its activity.

During Omaha's celebration of the vast Exposition, Bridget gave birth to a little girl, Julia Cecelia, born on July 9, 1898, in the front bedroom of their home on U Street. Michael couldn't contain his excitement at having a daughter named Julia after his mother. He paid special attention to the rosy-cheeked baby and enjoyed any time he could have her all to himself. Though Bridget named the child Julia Cecelia to satisfy her husband, she would be calling the baby Cecelia, the name she preferred. Bridget's prominent role as matriarch was never challenged. Michael admired the way in which she governed the family, so Cecelia it was!

Every morning, Bridget packed Michael's lunch in an empty lard bucket, and every Saturday night Michael took that empty bucket to the saloon. That was the night when he enjoyed not only the brew but also the good company of his friends. The family brewed their own beer on many occasions, and each of the children was offered a taste, but only after Michael stuck a hot poker into it to burn away the alcohol.

1900-02

Another son was born on September 20th in the home on U Street. Michael chose the name Carberry in remembrance of the Ballycarberry Castle in Cahersiveen. Growing up, Michael had loved to swim in the water surrounding the ancient ruin. Everyone wondered why he would tag his son with such an unusual name. Whatever the reason, his son would grow to hate the name, Carberry.

A second daughter, Mary Elenore, was born on September 17, 1902, and was baptized in the new church of St. Mary's on Q Street.

The mild winter passed uneventfully and with the spring, Bridget planted a variety of vegetables. She hired a laundress so that she could have more time to tend to their large family. Michael constructed an outdoor laundry area behind the chicken coop where he installed a hand pump and large iron sinks. A wooden washboard and wringer stood nearby. She had never completely adjusted to the pungent aroma of the stockyards, and she was further assaulted by the Stink "Crik" that flowed a few blocks from their home. Stockyard workers dumped animal renderings into the creek each week, and when the creek dried up, the dreadful smell gripped the entire county. The children were used to the odor, and she swore that Michael's sense of smell had left him years ago.

Time had stolen many of Bridget's precious memories of Valentia, and the untold grief of losing two young children further wounded her heart. She wondered just how much pain she could endure and often felt that the saints in heaven had abandoned her. Sometimes, holding the dried heather and gorse from Ballyhearney, she remembered her cottage in Ireland rooted amidst emerald green fields nourished by the gentle rain. In comparison, the home on U Street was built in a mud field, and the haze from industrial smokestacks spewed grime and soot on their windowsills. Images of her childhood past were dulled by the difficulties she endured in the present.

1904

Sons John and James found work as laborers, while Thomas, Francis, Cecelia, and Carberry attended the new Corrigan School. In the early fall and spring, the children went to school barefoot in order to save wear on the one pair of boots they owned. Schoolyard fights occurred often, and in winter the children would wrap snow around rocks to use as weapons. Bridget doled out many a punishment to her sons for participating in these battles, though she failed to understand the reason for some of the fights. Thomas and Francis fought to protect their brother Carberry, whose unusual name provided the spark to ignite many after-school brawls. Unfortunately, the principal paddled the boys, and Bridget continued to discipline them. Carberry couldn't wait for the day when he could change his name to something else, for any name would be better than "Carb."

Hannora Catherine was the first Shea baby to be born in a hospital. She entered the world on May 30th under the artificial lights of the delivery room. Bridget insisted that this baby, very well her last, be born in the sterile environment of a modern ward.

The harsh winter found each of the Shea children suffering from one cold or another, and Catherine became weak from the croup. The doctor prescribed cool baths to keep her fever down. Michael and Bridget held her all night, taking turns wringing the cool rag for her fevered brow.

Catherine slipped away on the night of February 25th at the age of nine months. Clutching the silent infant to her breast, Bridget refused to give her up. When she finally released the stilled bundle into Michael's care, she felt her own heart shatter into a million tiny pieces.

Neighbors and friends came to mourn the child's unexpected death and to offer their condolences. For Bridget and Michael who had suffered so greatly the pain of losing another child, there could be no comfort. Sitting beside each other, their sobs could be heard echoing throughout their small home. Rosaries dangled from their arthritic fingers, the ancient rough beads worn smooth from years of prayer, years of begging for God's grace and mercy. Surrounded by their grieving children, they offered prayers for their baby's innocent soul.

Bridget left Michael's side for a moment. When she returned, she placed a tattered hanky in Catherine's tiny palm. Caressing the delicate fingers, she found comfort in knowing that the heather and gorse would be with her baby for all eternity.

The tiny wooden coffin arrived at St. Mary's Cemetery in a fine horse-drawn carriage. Catherine joined her brothers Daniel and Michael under the sturdy, young oak nourished by their presence.

CHAPTER 21

Sturdy and Strong

November 1911-1913

The tiny American flag carried home from the Courthouse leaned against the steaming bowl of oxtail soup. Thick slices of homemade brown bread, platters of meat, potatoes, and vegetables covered the table. Today was a day to celebrate; Michael and Bridget were finally true American citizens. It had taken twenty-one years and one failed attempt, but today they were finally free from all ties to England. Michael raised his glass and thanked all the saints in heaven for the hard-won gift.

Bridget rested, exhausted from her day. Climbing in and out of their horse cart had not been easy, her left leg ached and seemed to have doubled in size since the morning. She reached for her glass of beer so they could share their triumph. Lifting the frosty glass to her parched lips, she sipped and enjoyed the taste of the brew.

Without money for gifts or store-bought cakes, celebrations were rare occasions. And the family were still suffering the sorrow of baby Catherine's death. Seven years had passed, but the little dresses and bonnets were still stored in a drawer of the large dresser.

When their oldest son, John, married, the family gathered for the sacred Mass and reception afterwards that was held in the church hall. Bridget remembered that evening well. It was just about that time she noticed the burning sensation in her left leg, but she dismissed it and promised herself that she would rest whenever possible.

The family no longer needed the services of a laundress. Cecelia and Mary helped their mother with that chore. Washing clothes was a major event usually taking two days to complete. Numerous pots of boiling water were carried out to the yard and poured into the washtubs, so the clothes could soak. In the winter when it was too cold to work outside, the clothes soaked in the kitchen sink. Cecelia and Mary rubbed and scrubbed them on metal washboards and wrung out every piece before hanging it on the line. Bridget taught Cecelia to use the flat iron. Mary watched enviously; she couldn't wait for the opportunity to try the new appliance, but Mary was only nine and Bridget worried that she would burn herself. Besides, she did a good job of hanging the wash out to dry.

Bridget's responsibilities grew as time passed. Even though the children helped, she carried the burden of managing the household. She mended the clothes, prepared three meals a day, and filled the stove with firewood. Her boys made sure to pile the wood close to the door so she wouldn't have to go out in the rain or icy weather. She also made the family's garments, and in the spring and fall she preserved fruits and vegetables. As much as she would have liked more time to rest, it just wasn't possible.

Bridget looked older than her forty-five years. Strands of gray streaked her dark hair and lines etched her translucent skin, weathered and worn from the harsh Nebraska climate. Every bone in her body ached. Her gait slowed by early afternoon, and standing at the stove for any length of time sapped all of her strength.

When the girls helped with the cooking and cleaning, Bridget sought the temporary warmth of the coal stove. Carberry sat close to her and read stories from his favorite book, *The Adventures of Tom Sawyer*. She frequently closed her eyes while listening to the sounds of his sweet voice. He was such a blessing to her, as were all her children, but there was something about Carberry that reminded her of her husband Michael. Carberry's devotion to her, along with his concern, touched her. Some of the words in the book were difficult, but he sailed over them with the ease of a scholar. His brown eyes danced with delight when he gained her approval.

Michael noticed the condition of Bridget's leg. The skin over her calf had turned bright red and was warm to his touch. He insisted she see a doctor, but Bridget would have none of that. Sure it was the rest she needed and promised to look after herself. She sought relief with patent medicines advertised in the numerous catalogs and newspapers she read. She also tried lots of old fashioned home remedies. She applied poultices of hot potatoes to her leg and took spoonfuls of blue flag root added to a pint of good spirits three times daily. Additional cures calling for mixtures of eggs, tar, soot, and other household ingredients were described on the pages of popular magazines. Bridget tried them all, without success.

Cecelia's thirteenth birthday approached and, though celebrations were rare, Bridget couldn't let that special day go by unnoticed. She wanted to mark her daughter's coming of age with a special gift. It had taken Bridget months to save up enough money to purchase a store bought gift, and she knew how much pleasure it would bring her daughter.

That evening the family gathered around the dining room table for a meal of roasted chicken, boiled potatoes, and turnips. After dinner, Bridget presented Cecelia with a small brown paper parcel tied with hemp string. Cecelia carefully pulled the paper away. She gasped in surprise and delight when she saw the small blue cloth-bound book entitled "Sturdy and Strong." It was the most beautiful gift Cecelia had ever received.

Bridget said that the story in the book reminded her of their struggles. Then she told them about her and Michael's desperate journey to America and how they stood sturdy and strong, facing their challenges with strength and courage. Her face glowed when she spoke about their lives in New London. The children, happy to see a smile on their mother's face, wished the evening would never end—it was a rare event that brought joy to the house on U Street.

One frosty November morning, a letter arrived from her family in Connecticut. It had been a long time since she'd heard anything from them and wondered what the news was. She unloosened the flap and slid the thin paper sheets from the envelope. Her eyes focused on each word as though it were a gift from the heavens. But her delight in receiving the letter turned into a sorrowful event. Her mother, Mary, had died in the cottage on Ballyhearney. Bridget was alone in the house. The only sounds that could be heard came from her—the sadness tore at her heart and further weakened her spirit. She wondered how her father was getting on and if he even remembered her.

As time passed, Bridget knew her family was hiding their concern from her, and she feared that her inability to manage the everyday responsibilities was an undue hardship for all of them.

The New Year brought a blessed addition to the family. A little girl was born to John and his wife. Bridget searched her granddaughter's face for any sign of resemblance to her own deceased child Catherine. At the baptism, she asked Father Mugan to bless the child who carried Catherine's spirit.

It wasn't long before Bridget could no longer get out of bed. Household chores were neglected and evening meals consisted of whatever Mary and Cecelia could throw together. Bridget finally relented and asked Michael to call the doctor.

She attempted to explain what hurt but could say only that her left leg felt hot; it burned, and the sharp pain ran from her calf up to her thigh. The doctor diagnosed her condition as varicose veins. The solutions he offered were medication, surgery, or vein injections. He insisted she choose one of the three because if she continued to neglect herself, the condition would worsen. The doctor further explained the condition was the result of her ten pregnancies, plus the additional burden of tending to her large family.

They discussed the options and decided to try the medication. She faithfully ingested the medicine prescribed, but her condition didn't improve. The pain in her leg became more intense, and she was desperate for relief.

The doctor explained that the surgery was a simple procedure. There had been some impressive scientific advances in the field of vein surgery, and he was sure that Bridget's condition could be cured.

Surgery was scheduled for December 2nd. Michael and the children assured her they could handle the chores at home while she recuperated. The parish priest prayed the rosary along with the family and placed her in God's hands. The surgeon accompanied her to the operating room and administered the chloroform.

The cold, white-tiled waiting room offered little encouragement to the family. A row of hard-backed wooden chairs lined the far wall, while a group of heavy-paned windows offered a view of the snow filled streets. Snow crystals draped thick tree branches that scratched at the windows with each gust of wind.

The children passed the time by watching out the windows at the horse drawn carriages that slipped and skidded their way down the icy streets. Michael paced the dull, green linoleum floor.

As the hours dragged on, the younger children snoozed, the older boys worried, and Michael continued to pace. Suddenly, the door opened. Rubbing the sleep from their eyes, Mary, Carberry, and Cecelia feigned alertness, while Francis, Thomas, James, and John stood close to their father.

Michael could tell by the look on Doctor Humpal's face that something was wrong. In that second, their lives changed forever.

A blood clot had killed Bridget. The doctor explained that during the surgery, a small piece of the blood clot in her leg had broken off. It lodged in her lungs, and she died from a lack of oxygen. His mumbled condolences and apologies fell on deaf ears: they were all in shock. The light in their lives had been extinguished, and they themselves felt dead.

Michael closed his eyes, wishing to shut out the pain. Life had been difficult in America, and he wondered what their lives would have been like if he'd met her in Valentia, if they had married and stayed in Ireland. Would God have been more merciful? Though he felt guilty for doubting God's love and mercy, Michael had to question why Bridget was taken from him.

Their sons made the funeral arrangements because Michael was unable to function. He hadn't spoken a word since Bridget's death. The body was waked in the living room on U Street. Neighbors and friends crowded into the little house, all offering their most sincere sympathies. Michael sat next to the casket while his children prayed for their mother's soul. He found little comfort in their prayers.

Carberry's happiness left him on the day the doctor announced his mother's death. Confused and angry, he wanted to run screaming from the house and continue running until he collapsed and died. He was only thirteen, and he needed her. It wasn't fair.

Bridget was laid to rest in St. Mary's Cemetery on a cold December morning. She joined her children Daniel, Michael, and Catherine alongside the oak tree whose long, sinewy branches promised shade during the unbearably hot Omaha summers.

CHAPTER 22

Unraveling

1913-1925

The familiar ticking of the old wall clock echoed throughout the house. Its steady rhythm offered solace with each swing of the pendulum. Michael remembered the day it arrived. Their son John had received it as a gift from his boss and proudly presented it to his mother. The family couldn't recall ever having seen her so surprised. She went on about that clock to anyone who cared to listen and insisted it be hung so that everyone who came through the back door could see it.

Michael reached across the table to pick up a magazine. Bridget had loved to read and looked forward to nights when she could sit with a cup of tea and catch up on the changing times and styles. He had argued that fifteen cents could buy more practical things than such foolishness as a Good Housekeeping magazine. Now he wished he could take back those words. When he pushed the magazine away, her faded picture fluttered to the floor. The pain and surprise of seeing her face overwhelmed him.

Hearing her father's cry, Cecelia rushed into the room.

He hadn't been able to express his grief before, and this sudden outburst frightened her. She picked up the picture she had hidden underneath the magazine earlier that morning, before the funeral. She was now angry with herself for being so inconsiderate. It had been her intention to put it back into the cabinet, but in all the confusion, she placed it, instead, underneath the magazine and out of the way. Uncomfortable with his outpouring of grief, she placed the picture on the table and left the room.

The snapshot, taken on their visit to the Omaha Exposition, showed her excitement at viewing the exhibits, and Michael remembered how important it was to her that their children understand the significance of the event. Curling his fingers around the photo, he wondered if he had ever told Bridget how much he loved her and how he couldn't imagine a life without her.

Moonlight sliced a path across the oilcloth-covered table and cast eerie shadows on the walls. Dishes were stacked in anticipation of an evening meal that went unprepared.

The younger children had told their mother they could handle things at home while she recuperated in the hospital. Why hadn't they told her they couldn't get along without her, that no one could ever take her place? Lying on her bed, Cecelia and Mary clutched her pillow, the slipcover, and stroked her worn nightgown until their sobs gave way to the relief of sleep.

The sons and John's wife gathered around the dining room table, unable to believe their precious mother was dead. After the funeral, they'd walked home in the blizzard, unable to feel the slush that oozed into their worn leather boots. By the time they reached their front door, they were soaked from the heavy snow. Silently, they filed into the house with no idea of what to do next. They were hungry, cold, and lonely for the sound of their mother's voice.

John's wife, Alice, weak from a recent bout of pneumonia wasn't feeling well and, in fact, hadn't been feeling well for quite some time. Alice knew her place was at her husband's side, and she grieved the loss as if it were her own mother who died.

Everywhere they looked, Bridget remained. White, black, and navy colored thread trailed from inside her sewing basket next to a small stack of socks that needed mending. A long, black woolen shawl hanging on a hook by the door still held the scent of her. Her worn prayer book was on the table near her rocking chair, the same chair in which she had rocked all her babies to sleep. Each of Bridget's children suffered their own personal grief, unable to share their sorrow even with each other.

Now they understood how uncertain life could be, and years later they would come to realize that Bridget's sudden death was the beginning of the family's unraveling.

1914

Michael pushed open the back door. He was thankful for his twelve-hour workdays; they kept him from thinking about Bridget. Hearing his children's cries, he dropped his lunch bucket on the kitchen table and hurried into the dining room. There he found them consoling their brother John. Cecelia told their father that Alice had unexpectedly died that afternoon of complications from pneumonia, leaving John alone with two young daughters. Michael collapsed into a chair. All he could do was shake his head and ask God, "Why!" He was sure they had suffered enough.

Alice had been taken to the hospital when she complained of a tightening in her chest. The doctors told John she would be fine, that all she needed was bed rest. Since they lived across the state line in Iowa, the distance made communication difficult. No one in Omaha knew how sick she really was, nor did they know that John needed help with the children.

With no one to care for them, John had no choice but to place them in an orphanage. He knew if his mother were alive, she would have taken them in and raised them as her own. But since her death, and now his wife's, John felt abandoned and alone.

Michael was disappointed with John's decision but could offer little help. He prayed to all the saints in heaven to watch over his little grandchildren, who would be raised by the Catholic nuns.

A few months later, James, at the age of twenty-seven, announced his plans to marry. Michael was happy to hear the news. There had been so much sadness in the family that a wedding celebration might be what they all needed.

After the ceremony, James and his wife, Ann, moved into a rented house nearby. James was planning to build a new home on the lot next door to his father's house. James was a State Claim Agent for the Union Pacific Railroad, and the job kept him out of town for weeks at a time; it comforted him to know that both families would look out for each other in his absence.

1916

Time was moving agonizingly slowly for Michael. The only thing that helped was the pride he felt for his children. He enjoyed their company and encouraged their visits. His son Thomas, now twenty-four, had been promoted to the position of Secretary for the Omaha Merchants' Association, and son Francis, who was nineteen, joined his father at Swift & Company as a steamfitter. But little had changed in Michael's day-to-day life. He continued to miss Bridget. He had no one to share in his joy or to help endure the sorrows that strained the family's lives.

Cecelia, eighteen, and Mary, fourteen, worked hard to keep the family going. After school, Mary scrubbed the laundry and hung the clothes out to dry. In the winter, the clothesline hung above the kitchen stove. Their mother had never left clothes on the line, but Mary didn't seem to have the time to take down the worn, unmended clothing. Bridget had made sure that each of her children was clean and well fed before leaving for school or work. Now they were messy, unwashed, and undernourished.

Cecelia walked to the streetcar every morning to ride into Omaha. She worked at Brandeis Dept. Store, earning only pennies per day for lifting heavy bolts of fabric and cutting European cotton and Chinese silk for the fancy ladies who shopped at their leisure. She worked long hours to save enough money to afford a good pair of shoes and store bought clothes. Times were tough since John, James, and Thomas moved out. Mary and Francis, with help from their younger brother Carberry, somehow managed.

One of Carberry's jobs was to walk to the market whenever they were low on supplies. He never minded doing this for his mother, but he didn't like his sisters bossing and constantly nagging. His unusual name only added to his distress. He asked that they call him by his middle name, Mike, but they refused. They reminded him how important it was to their mother that he not change his name. Michael was the name of their little baby brother who had died. This only frustrated him further. He didn't want to go through life with the horrible nickname "Carb," and now that he was sixteen, out of school, and working at the stockyards, it was time to tell his father of his decision.

Michael was furious. Changing his name was one thing, but taking the name of his deceased brother was another. Michael pleaded with his son, calling on the boy's sainted mother to intervene in such foolishness. Headstrong and determined, Carberry told his family that he was to be known as Mike, and that Carberry would be his middle name. His father warned him of heartache and misfortune. Surely it was bad luck to take the name. And what would they tell the good priest at St. Mary's?

The pastor at St. Mary's Church greeted the Shea family after every Sunday Mass. Father Mugan continued to include them in his prayers. Looking over the congregation, he wondered why Carberry no longer attended Mass. The priest knew that ever since the death of his mother, Carberry continued to ignore the teachings of his faith, and as much as he tried to convince him to attend Mass, Carberry would have none of it.

1919

Mary stopped to pray each morning on the way to her job at the telephone company. Of all Bridget's children, she was the one most likely to choose the religious life. And since her mother's death, the only time she felt at peace was when she prayed. She decided to enter the order of the Daughters of the Heart of Mercy but not until her father could do without her help at home. One evening after dinner, Mary announced her interest in one day joining the convent. The family was pleased with the news and happy about her decision. Michael was proud that one of his children would enter the service of the church.

Carberry couldn't believe what he heard. How could she consider giving her life to a God who took their mother from them? It was then he knew he could no longer live in his family's home. Six years had passed since her death, yet he continued to mourn her. Since she died, he could not recall being really happy.

Carberry heard that the packinghouses in Chicago were thriving, and with his experience as a clerk at Swift & Company, he was confident that he could secure an office job there. Grunt work didn't interest him. For too many years, he had watched his father grow old from the harsh weather and tough work of the yards.

On a fine summer morning, Carberry walked away from his family in South Omaha, and he never looked back.

1920

Cecelia married and moved to Kansas City with her husband. Later, when her daughter was born, she asked her father to join them; she could use his help. Michael accepted because he needed to feel useful, and his job as plant foreman at the packinghouse no longer interested him. He sold the house on U Street to his son James for $2,250, packed his few belongings, and moved to Kansas City.

1923

From Kansas City, Missouri, Cecelia's husband moved the family to Potwin, Kansas, and her father moved with them. Michael tried to find something pleasant about Potwin, but he couldn't adjust to life there. He experienced prejudice from the neighbors; being Irish and Catholic didn't make him the most popular newcomer. He missed the company of his Irish friends in South Omaha, and he decided to go back. Now he was ready to face the memories he had traveled so far away from to forget.

James and Ann welcomed Michael into their home on U Street. They tried to make him feel comfortable, but Michael wanted only to be left alone. Thinking he would enjoy seeing his old friends, James arranged for a small gathering at the house. It was a good effort, but Michael continued to retreat into himself.

Most days he napped in the thick cushioned side chair. Other times he walked to the saloon on 36th & V Street to play cards with the retirees who, like himself, didn't have much to do. And as always, he missed Bridget.

1924

Michael's sixty-sixth birthday passed without fuss. His children were scattered and busy with their own lives.

Though he was grateful he had found a home with James and Ann, it was difficult to live next door to the house he had purchased with Bridget.

He hadn't felt good for months but put off going to the doctor. One morning he felt an odd tugging on the right side of his face, and his mouth twisted uncontrollably into a crooked grimace. He felt weak and his words were jumbled. Alarmed, James rushed his father to the hospital. The doctor said Michael had had a mild stroke and sent him home to recuperate. Ann welcomed him home with oxtail soup and homemade brown bread. She was sure it was just the thing to bring a smile to his sober face.

1925

Michael woke early on a beautiful April morning when the sun was just rising over the horizon. Robins chirped their spring arrival, and the driver of the milk wagon slowed, taking time to enjoy the warm breezes. Michael's recovery was going well. The doctor was pleased with his progress. He walked with the aid of a cane and suffered only slight discomfort from the effects of his stroke. Nevertheless, he felt helpless, old, and lonely, and wondered what his end would be.

Walking gave him time to think. He was grateful for his children and memories of his life with Bridget. He often wondered what their lives would have been like had they stayed in Connecticut. Would their three children, now buried next to Bridget, have survived? Were their deaths caused by the hardships the family had endured? In Connecticut they had extended family. In Omaha they had only each other. Michael knew that Bridget never liked living in South Omaha. The smell, the dirt, the loneliness, the hard work—that was all she had to look forward to every day, yet, she did what was expected of her and never complained.

Michael headed in the direction of St. Mary's Cemetery. Consumed with thoughts of Bridget, he followed the path to her grave. As if being pulled, his pace quickened. Collapsing at her grave, he sobbed without restraint.

That afternoon James received a call from Thomas. The police requested they come to the station as quickly as possible. A fisherman had found a body in the Missouri River around noon, and they needed a positive identification.

After identifying the body, James and Thomas walked to the river and to the place where their father's body was found. As much as they anguished over his sudden death, they felt strangely at peace, comforted with the thought that their father would no longer suffer the pain of his ailments or continue to grieve the loss of his beloved wife.

The banks of the Missouri River are steep in the area near the Sarpy County Line, and the river runs rough. They were sure that he had tripped on the tangled tree roots hidden by spring's new growth. They could see how he might have tumbled into the river.

The gray enamel casket adorned with a large crucifix sat in the living room in James's home on U Street. Father Hallinan and Father Mugan prayed the rosary along with family, friends, and neighbors. Carberry was noticeably absent.

The horse-drawn hearse wound its way into St. Mary's Cemetery; Michael was laid to rest next to his lovely Irish girl and close to his three children: Daniel, Michael, and Catherine. With his body safe beside Bridget, their spirits were free to find their way to the lush green fields of Ireland, to those mountains and valleys filled with the delicate wildflowers of their youth.

Grandparents
Married: February 17, 1885

MICHAEL SHEA
Born: November 15, 1859
                  Townland of Carhan Lower
                  Cahersiveen,
                      County Kerry, Ireland

Emigrated: August 30, 1880
Departed: Queenstown, Ireland
Arrived: Castle Gardens, New York
Resided: Connecticut and Nebraska
Died: April 10, 1925

BRIDGET MURPHY
Born: January 15, 1865
                  Townland of Ballyhearney
                  Valentia Island,
                    County Kerry, Ireland

Emigrated: May 15, 1880
Departed: Queenstown, Ireland
Arrived: Castle Gardens, New York
Resided: Connecticut and Nebraska
Died: December 2, 1913

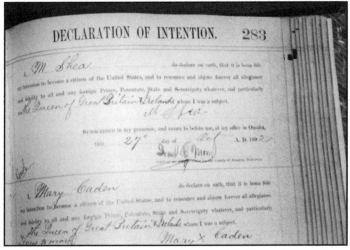

Recorded Declaration of Intent for Michael and Bridget to become U.S. citizens—Omaha, Nebraska   October 27, 1892

Ballycarberry Castle, Cahersiveen, County Kerry, Ireland   2004

The Sturdy and Strong *book given in celebration of Cecelia's 13th birthday from her mother, Bridget in 1911*

The Shea home on U Street in Omaha, Nebraska (recently remodeled)

CHAPTER 23

Emigration of Sarah Beirne and Michael Healy Boyle, County Roscommon, Ireland

May 1903

Strong winds pounded the little cottage on Ardmoyle and torrential rains soaked the thatched roof. Streaks of lightning pierced the afternoon sky. The walls leaked moisture from hairline cracks that webbed the clay interior. Sparks jumped from the peat fire crackling in the hearth. The strong smell of boiling potatoes, mixed with the smoky aroma of the open fire, permeated the tiny cottage.

The three Beirne children huddled around the fire, waiting for their dinner. One of their four chairs was propped up against the front door to secure it against the blustery winds. The list of repairs grew daily. They could barely keep up with the rent payments and couldn't make the necessary repairs to the cottage. Daniel, twenty-five;

Sarah, eighteen; and Elizabeth, fifteen had grown restless waiting for the letter with the money for their passage to America to arrive.

On September 21, 1896, six months after the onset of the cough, their mother Mary had died. On March 19, 1897, their father, John, succumbed to a cough that had plagued him for years. Frightened and unsure of their future, the children stayed together in spite of the odds against them. They had scraped together what little money they had saved so that their siblings Patrick, twenty-one, and Anne, twenty-three, could go to America.

Anne had left the cottage on Ardmoyle in 1902. Sarah remembered her sister taking the good, sturdy boots they had shared and their mother's warm woolen shawl. Elizabeth didn't mind Anne packing the boots and shawl into her case. They didn't fit her, for she was much smaller than her sisters.

Anne and Sarah took after their father, who was short and stocky. Elizabeth inherited her mother's looks; she was small and delicate and required more rest than the others. Being the baby of the family, Elizabeth enjoyed everyone's attention. Sarah resented the special treatment given to her younger sister, and she disliked having to wait on her.

After their parents died, the Beirne children became responsible not only for their own survival but also for the health and well being of each other. When Patrick and Anne emigrated to Chicago, Sarah took charge of the household. The burden proved too much for her, and each day brought her further into despair.

Daniel found trouble around every corner and acquired the reputation for being a ruffian. Work around the farm piled up, while Daniel sought comfort from the company of his peers at the Kingsland Pub. He tried to convince his sister that a good card game and a couple of drinks would lift his spirits. After all, hadn't they suffered enough since the death of their parents? Sarah watched the little bit of money they had managed to save dwindle away. She was tired of looking after her brother and sister and knew if she didn't leave Ireland soon, her life would be wasted.

Michael Healy had proposed marriage to Sarah. He was twenty years old and lived down the road on Carrowkeel. Michael's father didn't approve of his son's plan to marry one of the Beirne girls. At the age of ninety-seven, William Healy needed one of his sons to marry a woman with a dowry so that rent money for the cottage could be guaranteed. Sarah Beirne was poor. She had nothing to bring to the marriage. Since Michael had no farm and Sarah, no dowry, neither of them would be able to marry while they lived in Ireland. Michael thought only of his lovely Sarah and the time when they would be man and wife. Together, they planned their journey across the sea.

Michael's brother John, who was twenty-one, had emigrated to Bridgeport, Connecticut in 1902. Every day, Michael and Sarah hoped the letters would arrive from each of their brothers with money for their passage.

William worried about his son and wondered how Michael could love a woman who longed for expensive things. He had agreed to his children's plan to leave Ireland only because he knew they deserved better than to grow old on the farm. Life here was hard work with little promise. He tried to convince Michael to stay in Bridgeport with his brother and sister after he arrived in America, but

Michael wouldn't hear of it. He made clear his intention to travel from Bridgeport to Chicago to be with Sarah.

Michael still suffered from his mother's death. Her soft voice and loving manner lingered in every corner of their cottage. Tears came easily when he thought back to the afternoon of May 1896 when she died. She had never complained and worked harder than most women because her husband was nearly forty years older. She relied on her sons to do the heavy work, though they had to attend school. As a result, she bore the brunt of the responsibility of tending to the farm as well as caring for her family. The burden proved to be too much, and she died from the pain in her stomach. She was fifty-two years old. Michael remembered his mother's face twisted in agony while the family prayed the rosary for her recovery. Talk in town was that the cancer took her.

Sarah was happy to have found someone who loved her. Michael was a good man and he spent a great deal of time at Sarah's cottage helping with the heavy work—man's work! Sarah looked at her large calloused hands and wondered if she would ever become the lady she wanted to be. She worried that her wide ugly feet would never fit into the neat little high-buttoned shoes that she once saw in a magazine. Sarah caught glimpses of herself in store windows when she went to town to sell butter and eggs. Dark hollow eyes stared back at her. But Michael always reassured Sarah of her beauty, even though it was apparent only to him.

The letters containing the money for passage finally arrived at the Boyle Post. Michael's brother John sent money for him and his sister Maggie to join him in

Bridgeport. Two weeks later, the money to pay ship passage for Sarah, Daniel, and Elizabeth arrived from Chicago. After waiting for over a year, the young people could finally pack for America.

Sarah carefully tucked her mother's three china plates, two wooden scoops, and a feather tick pillow into her bundle. The hem of her only dress was frayed and ragged from wear. Her old leather boots pinched her toes, causing her to wince in pain with each step. She silently cursed her older sister for robbing her of the comfortable boots. Daniel and Elizabeth bundled their few belongings in the blankets.

Sarah lingered on the bed where her parents had died six years before; she remembered it as though it were yesterday. Her tears dampened her wool shawl. She needed her mother to wish them well on their journey. Since her mother's death, she had felt empty inside, as though a part of her had died as well. Leaving Ireland had seemed like such a good idea, but now she found herself worrying if she would fit in and if she could ever really love Michael. The day Sarah prayed for had finally arrived. She was leaving Ardmoyle for a new life in America. Why wasn't she able to feel happy?

Michael and Maggie visited neighbors and spent their last hours with their father and seventeen year old brother Peter in the cottage on Carrowkeel. A mixture of gaiety and sorrow marked their departure as neighbors, family, and friends danced through the night at the traditional Irish "wake" of saying good-bye.

Michael slept later than he had intended. Maggie packed the items necessary for their voyage. She knew Michael would enjoy having some of their mother's things in the apartment in Bridgeport, so she also packed the cup from the top shelf that had gathered dust since her death. Maggie whispered a soft morning greeting to her brother and reminded him that the train would leave Boyle for Dublin in less than two hours.

William Healy leaned against the metal gate outside the tiny cottage. His thick hand supported the arm holding his pipe. He had lost his older son, John, to America, and today, he was losing another son and a daughter to the land beyond the sea. Michael was truly his mother's son, for his kind and genteel manner was his strongest quality. His lovely daughter Maggie meant the world to him. Her laughter and song brightened his lonely life. Two of his wives had died, and now the children that were leaving would be as good as dead to him as well. Thunder rumbled in the distance while the smoke from his pipe caught a breeze and disappeared into the air.

The Boyle train depot buzzed with excitement. Boxes tied with twine, furniture, and bundles were stacked on the platform, their owners placing them carefully out of the way of the children running between the piles. While Michael searched the crowd for Sarah, Maggie hugged her brother Peter good-bye and reminded him to take good care of himself and their father. Peter wished he were going with them for he knew he'd miss them more than any-thing—but someone had to stay back to care for the farm and their elderly father.

Sarah could be seen in the distance herding her brother and sister onto the platform. She barked instructions for them to stay with the bundles while she went in search of the Healy family.

Peter and Maggie watched Sarah as she scanned the area alongside the train, both of them not wanting to share their last moments with her. Maggie rolled her eyes and called on her dead mother for the strength it would take to spend a week with the likes of Sarah in the cramped steerage compartment of a ship. Maggie didn't trust Sarah, and Sarah thought that Maggie was overly protective of her brothers.

The cry of the conductor could be heard above the crowd—All Aboard for Dublin City. The two families found seats together in the crowded train. People packed the aisles and hung out the doors as the train chugged its way out of the depot. Hope, tempered with an overwhelming sense of loss weighed heavily in the hearts of the young emigrants. Having never journeyed from Boyle, the five young people watched in awe as the landscape changed from bog fields to crowded city streets. From Dublin, they would catch the next train to the port of Queenstown.

The White Star Shipping Line arranged for every emigrant to stay at a hotel for a few days before boarding their ships, they were required to deliver passengers who were free from disease, and if any were rejected and sent back to Ireland, the shipping companies would be fined one hundred dollars each plus the cost of the return journey. To avoid this costly situation, the shipping companies arranged for the steerage passengers to undergo de-lousing.

The hotels provided dormitory beds for the emigrants. While they stood under cold showers, their clothes were sprayed for lice. All their belongings were disinfected. After days of de-lousing, they were moved to the clean side of the hotel, where they were quarantined and given rations of food. Under no circumstances could they leave the hotel until their ship left for America.

The emigrants packed oatcakes and meal to last them for the week it would take for their journey to Ellis Island. Some of them had live chickens packed into ragged baskets and turf for the fires they'd make in the little stoves on deck. They were careful not to eat any of the food they packed for the voyage because it had to last the duration of the trip.

The young emigrants stood on heartbreak pier. Sounds of wind-swept waves lapping over the splintered wooden deck, the salty smell of the sea, and the mournful sobs of the women reminded the young emigrants of their own sadness at leaving their homeland.

Michael held Sarah's hand and a numbing fear gripped him. They focused on the huge ship that awaited them. Large smokestacks could be seen churning out white cloudy smoke.

Before boarding the tenders, each passenger was questioned and their belongings searched and documented. If they left Ireland with twenty-five dollars, they needed to arrive in New York with twenty-five dollars. Gambling on the ships was prohibited. Any person arriving without the money they left with would be considered a poor risk for America.

Families clung together for fear of being separated. The first and second-class passengers boarded, and then the steerage passengers entered the ship below the first and second-class staterooms. The conditions appeared extremely unpleasant, and Michael did his best to comfort Maggie, Sarah, and Elizabeth while helping them locate their berths and store their belongings. Meanwhile, to insure a quick trip to the deck, Sarah's brother Daniel claimed a double berth close to the door. If there were any card games or drinking, he would surely be there to try his luck and drown his sorrows.

When the steamship bellowed its intent to depart the shores of Ireland, thousands of emigrants went up on deck to hang over the rails for their final glimpse of their beloved island. Looking toward the shore, Michael noticed the laborers who were putting the finishing touches on the spires of the newly built St. Coleman's Cathedral. "Holy Mary, Mother of God," he prayed, "Protect us on our journey and deliver us safely to our destination." He reached into his jacket pocket for a handkerchief to catch his tears.

Clouds moved swiftly inland while the ship moved away from its mooring. Seagulls stood on the lifeboats, their feathers rustling in the wind. Tops of trees could be seen waving over the centuries-old buildings in a ceremonial farewell as the port disappeared from view.

The thundering waves pounding the steel bow kept everyone from sleeping. A number of times during the journey, Sarah was certain the ship had hit a rocky shore. How else could she account for the times she was tossed from her berth? The ship creaked and groaned throughout their harrowing journey.

When the rays of the rising sun warmed the deck, the steerage passengers came up to socialize around the makeshift stoves. Large air vents loomed overhead like majestic horns providing passage for the tired sea birds that nested along the way. Lifeboats, suspended by ropes and cables, rocked from the railings. Steam rose from huge towers on the port and starboard sides. Michael enjoyed the days on the sun-drenched deck. The cloudless blue skies offered hope for a new beginning.

He comforted Sarah during the voyage, telling her of the wonderful life waiting for them in America; he took care to keep her hopes alive and her spirit strong. Maggie hated to see her brother give up his meals to Sarah, who took them so willingly without any thought of Michael's well being.

The day they all looked forward to arrived! They could see Ellis Island in the distance, and the Statue of Liberty rising from the bottomless ocean. Passengers shouted, hanging onto the rails. They had never seen anything so beautiful in their lives. They were in America, where life was golden.

After entering the harbor, the steerage passengers spent several days on board the ship waiting to be cleared for entry. Then they were shuttled to shore on open barges in the deadly heat where they waited for hours; some of the elderly emigrants, already weakened from their voyage, died. Those who survived the journey across the ocean and the hours spent on a barge dropped to their knees and kissed the American soil.

White paper health certificates and identification tags hung on the jackets of all passengers. The numbers on the tags matched the numbers on the Passenger Manifest list. Michael and Maggie Healy were #49605 and the Beirne family #49604.

They were divided into groups of thirty. While the passengers proceeded to the main building, their baggage was dropped into a storage area for later retrieval. American volunteers carried trays of cold milk and raised donuts to the new immigrants, providing them with their first taste of America. The families welcomed the offering because food in their stomachs helped to soothe their weary bodies.

The young immigrants were surrounded by strangers and traumatized by the activity involved in their immigration processing. Tripping over cases and boxes, they were pushed and shoved to the staircase leading to the second floor. While they waited on the stairwell, they were inspected for breathing problems, strange behaviors, and difficulty walking or standing.

Blue chalk marks on the jackets of those waiting to be processed alerted the officials to problems, and they were pulled from the line. Checking for sixty symptoms of disease and fungus took minutes. This was frightening, as most of the immigrants had never been to a doctor in their lives. Buttonhooks, hairpins, and fingers were used to flip back the eyelids to check for trachoma. An immigrant could be rejected for any perceived threat of illness.

Individuals were also refused entrance if they failed a written test. Nine out of every hundred persons were held back, but they were allowed to take the test three times. If they were feeble minded, had poor hearing, or couldn't read and write, they were in danger of being rejected, unless their families could come to their aid and beg their cases.

Herded into the Registry Room, thousands of immigrants were separated from the other areas by iron bars and chicken wire. Heat rising from so many bodies nearly suffocated the weaker ones. The odor of perspiration mixed with the smell of the harbor was nauseating. The last ones to be questioned waited up to five hours. There were twenty-nine questions including name, age, occupation, and whether or not they were anarchists. The amount of money they left Ireland with had to be accounted for. All immigrants had to prove they were capable of working. In fact, they had to have jobs waiting for them upon their arrival, for they couldn't take jobs away from Americans.

Sarah, Daniel, and Elizabeth Beirne became Sarah, Daniel, and Elizabeth Burns. Mistakes were made in transcription, and who would dare to correct an official?

The final phase of processing included giving up their tags, checking the names of their sponsors, and finalizing their applications for approval to enter the United States. Once they had permission to leave Ellis Island, the immigrants found themselves at the Stairs of Separation. If the sponsoring family was not there to claim them, they would be detained until someone arrived to escort them away. No women would be allowed to leave Ellis Island unaccompanied for fear they might be sold into white slavery.

Sarah and Michael lingered at the kissing post. Michael promised to work hard to save enough money for his transportation to Chicago and for their marriage license.

Patrick and Anne Beirne were waiting for Sarah, Daniel, and Elizabeth to emerge from the holding area and rushed to greet them. Together they boarded the train to Chicago, Illinois.

John Healy ran into the arms of his sister Maggie and brother Michael and hugged them both. John had missed his brother and sister and found it difficult to leave their embrace. He could hardly believe they had finally arrived. After finding their bundles, they walked to the train bound for Bridgeport, Connecticut.

America held their dreams, for it was here they would realize opportunities unlike anything they could ever have imagined in Ireland. What they didn't realize was that they would be expected to work eighty-hour weeks for the sum of ten dollars per week. But that was a small price for freedom.

CHAPTER 24

Sarah Burns Settles In Chicago, Illinois

July 1903

Sarah and Elizabeth looked out the window as the train chugged its way to Chicago. This ride didn't provide views of thatched cottages nestled in small villages. Instead, it offered a new landscape—dense woods and wide plains divided by large industrial cities. It delighted them to see the majestic beauty of the towering pine forests. There were no forests in County Roscommon, for if there were, they could have burned wood rather than the peat from the bogs. Sarah's calloused hands bore the scars from years of slicing through the damp cold earth, digging up the fuel to cook their food and heat their cottage.

Horse drawn wagons and coaches stopped at crossing gates, waiting for the train to pass. There were one-horse carriages with tall, thin wheels and fancier ones with four enormous bay horses and an enclosed passenger coach. Patrick pointed out a horseless carriage called the Brewster Side Car, and they saw their first motor bicycle parked outside a train depot. Patrick was thrilled to be able to show them all the wonderful new things in America.

He spoke to his brother in both English and Irish because he had so much to tell him. Daniel listened carefully to each word; he was amazed and surprised at all he saw and heard. There was so much he wanted to know, but he couldn't think of where to begin his questions, so he let Patrick just go on telling about the city he was about to call home.

Anne sat curled up close to the window. Sarah thought her sister was distant, but then she remembered that Anne was never one to talk much, and Sarah wondered if they would ever be friends. Their mother used to call the two of them "old fish women" for all the bickering they did. Putting that uncomfortable memory aside, she began to think about what her life would be like in this new place. She already knew she needed new clothes and comfortable shoes. And, she had her wedding to plan.

Sarah looked down at her dingy, gray wool dress and felt poor and out of place. She wondered if Elizabeth noticed how different they looked from the other passengers. She closed her eyes and dreamed of having a pretty bedroom with lace curtains and a store-bought mattress. In her dream, she was surrounded with thick feather quilts and soft pillows. She imagined her closets bulging with fancy lace gowns, pretty floral cotton day dresses, linen blouses decorated with colored embroidery, long flowing skirts, cotton petticoats, and black leather high button boots. She trusted that Patrick had picked out a beautiful place for them to live in; after all, weren't the streets in America paved in gold?

They dozed and ate little during their thirteen hundred mile journey. Patrick hoped his brother and sisters would find their small tenement flat acceptable and comfortable. Anne would be moving out in the next couple of months because she had met a McDonough man and it looked as though they would be married soon. He knew that Sarah planned to marry Michael Healy as soon as he could move to Chicago, for he had overheard their plans before they parted at Ellis Island. Patrick had grown up with the Healy family down the road on Carrowkeel, and he knew them to be good people. Knowing his sister Sarah to be a handful, he hoped that Michael Healy was prepared for the likes of her. He figured that Elizabeth would meet someone after settling in: she was a looker and the sweetest of his sisters.

As their train neared the Chicago depot, they saw towering eight-storied skyscrapers lining the city streets, each one seeming to be more imposing than the other. Hissing steam rose from the underside of the locomotive, signaling the conductor to announce their arrival. The Burns children straightened their tattered clothing, gathered their ragged bundles, and followed Anne and Patrick into the depot. The cavernous train station looked nothing like the small depot in Boyle, and they were nearly knocked off their feet by the crowds of busy people who rushed past them.

Sarah clutched her bundle tightly to her chest for fear someone would grab it and run. She had never seen so many people in one place, and she recalled stories she'd heard about the thieves who ran rampant through large cities. Chicago was nothing like she expected.

Out on the street, the air smelled different, not fresh, and much like the smell that came from the rotted garbage in back of the Boyle Meat Market on sultry days. Sarah also recognized a fishy smell, the same kind that gagged her when she cleaned fish that Michael caught in the waters of Lough Gara outside Boyle.

The frenzied pace of the busy city rattled the three newcomers. They stayed close to Patrick and Anne for fear of being separated. Patrick attempted to explain all the new things his brother and sisters were seeing, but his voice was drowned out by the commotion. Bicycles, pushcarts, horse drawn vehicles, and electric streetcars crowded the avenues. The elevated train rumbled overhead, causing Sarah, Elizabeth, and Daniel to scream out loud, but no one noticed their frightened cries over the clatter of the city. They bumped into hurrying pedestrians who seemed to be outraged by their mere presence. Everything was new to them, and they gawked at everyone and everything in their line of vision.

The hot, humid summer air pressed against their lungs. Their cumbersome wool clothing, soaked with perspiration, and the weight of their heavy bundles made it difficult to walk. As they trudged through the congested city, they were surprised to hear so many different languages spoken by other immigrants carrying bundles. Sarah looked at them in horror. She hoped she didn't look so ragged and hopeless. But her brother and sister were also dressed in tattered clothing, and she was sure they appeared just as miserable as all the newly arrived immigrants who walked these city streets.

Patrick and Anne paused in front of the apartment building at 318 West Madison Street. Sarah was sure this couldn't be the right place because it was dirty and run-down. How could the beautiful bedroom she dreamed of be housed in such a dilapidated old building? Anne, seeing Sarah's surprise, reminded them how lucky they were to have a roof over their heads. Sarah said nothing, only holding back her tears of disappointment.

They waited patiently while Patrick fumbled for the key. The long hike from the train station had worn them out and now, having to climb three flights of stairs, they were ready to drop. The gloomy hallway reeked from unfamiliar odors. The wails of babies mingled with the caterwauling of the building's occupants startled the young immigrants. As Patrick struggled to insert the key into the rusted lock, he could feel Sarah's hot breath on his neck.

Sarah was first to enter the front room, and when all five of them stood there, they filled the room. Patrick suggested they let their eyes adjust to the darkness before walking around, so they dropped their bundles and collapsed on the floor. Anne told them that the front room would serve as Daniel and Patrick's bedroom, while the girls would share her room off the kitchen. Sarah was too tired to put up a fuss, but she was disappointed to see that the flat was smaller than their cottage in Ireland.

The kitchen could hold only two people at a time because the coal stove, kitchen sink, and icebox took up most of the space. They had never seen a sink in the kitchen—or an icebox, for that matter—and the three new immigrants expressed their amazement at having such wonderful things as running water and a cold box in which to store meat, milk, and vegetables. Daniel asked about the coal stove. Patrick explained they would have to haul the coal up from the yard to keep the fire burning so they could cook the meals and heat the flat. Sarah and Elizabeth asked where the hearth was. Anne laughed and told them they would be doing all the cooking on top of the coal stove. Sarah bit her tongue to keep from telling Anne that it would be a cold day in hell that she'd be cooking for her. Patrick quickly changed the subject by mentioning that the toilet was located underneath the back hallway stairs. Sarah and Elizabeth were mortified to think that they would have to bare their *arses* to the entire building. Patrick put their fears to rest by explaining the kickboards behind the steps would give them the privacy they desired. Daniel laughed out loud, thinking of his sisters balancing themselves on the back steps. Then it dawned on him that he, too, would be straddling the stairs.

Patrick paid seven dollars per month rent and was happy to have found a clean place, for many of the other tenements in the city were infested with rats and roaches. He worked sixty hours a week as a laborer, digging ditches and pouring concrete for the annual wage of six hundred dollars. Anne worked as a servant when the rich needed extra help for their parties.

Sarah went into the front room and stood looking out the window at the city below. Her brother hadn't done as well as she thought, and she reminded herself that one of her reasons for leaving Ireland was to escape their poverty. She had set her sights on a life filled with beautiful things. Her goals were loftier than Patrick's, and she decided at that moment to separate herself from her family as soon as the time was right. Then she thought of Michael Healy and wondered what he was doing in Bridgeport and how soon he could come to marry her.

CHAPTER 25

City Girl Sarah Burns

September 1903

Sarah welcomed September's breezes. Chicago had been hot and humid, and she had thought the August heat would suffocate her. She spent most of her time outside, wandering the city and becoming familiar with all the new sights. For a nickel she could ride the trolley to the end of the line, or visit Duchess the elephant at the Lincoln Park Zoo. Sarah had never seen such an enormous animal. Lions, tigers, leopards, jaguars, and hyenas moved freely between the inside and outside cages. There were no wild animals in Ireland except the fox, and it seemed the fox was milder-mannered than the exotic animals she saw at the zoo. She sat for hours thinking about the kinds of places those animals came from.

When she could talk her sister and brothers into going to the park in the evenings, they enjoyed music performed by live orchestras. When the revelers got up to dance, Sarah looked over at the young men and wondered if one of them would approach and ask her to dance with him. But it didn't happen. Sitting next to Elizabeth, she felt dowdy and unattractive. Elizabeth was the beauty in the family. Every man turned in admiration. Sarah thought if she could be as pretty and as tiny as her sister, then she could pick any man she wanted.

Sarah expected that Michael Healy would arrive soon from Bridgeport, Connecticut to marry her. At least, that's what he said in his letter. She was already impatient with him because she needed to move out of the crowded tenement her brother had rented. Life was a little easier since Anne got married—at least she didn't have to clean up after her any longer. Even so, the small apartment was still overcrowded.

Anne married well and already owned a house with a bathtub and flush toilets. Steam hissed from the radiators and thick oriental carpets graced the hallway. Sarah wanted a house and all the fine things that Anne had. Since Anne left, she hadn't even come back to visit. They were invited into her home for a party after the church ceremony, but Sarah knew they were an embarrassment to Anne. Sarah wasn't surprised. Anne had always seen herself as better than the rest of them.

Patrick worried about Daniel. He couldn't hold on to a job, and he kept company with an unscrupulous bunch of characters. Patrick warned him about them, but Daniel continued his descent into the gutters of the city. Many a night Patrick had to come and carry his brother home from one of the saloons on Madison Street.

Elizabeth's favorite activity was walking the few blocks from their home to State Street to gaze in the windows of the Marshall Field's store. Known as the Palace of Desire, Field's catered almost exclusively to women. Window-shopping on State Street offered them an escape from the drudgery of children, cleaning, cooking, and sewing. Sarah criticized her younger sister for looking at things in store windows she couldn't buy. She had read that many priests and politicians disapproved of the "peep shows," warning that they bred loose behavior and destroyed contentment. Sarah had all she could do to keep Daniel in line without having to worry about Elizabeth. Elizabeth resented Sarah's hypocritical attitude, for she knew that Sarah also longed to have the beautiful things on display in those windows.

The Chicago American newspaper advertised for clerks to work in the Field's store. Straightening her long wool skirt, Elizabeth checked her reflection in the plate glass window. Once she stepped through the doors of the glittery retail world, she found herself wanting things she'd never even seen before that very moment. She approached a clerk to inquire about a job.

The clerk directed her to offices on the third floor. When Elizabeth walked into the waiting room, she noticed other girls filling out forms. Determined to leave with a job, Elizabeth approached the desk and asked for an application. After a three-hour wait, she was called in for the interview and was hired.

As a salesgirl at Field's, Elizabeth earned six dollars a week. If she saved her money, she could buy one or two ready-to-wear outfits that would instantly place her on a level with her middle-class customers. She knew it was possible to move up in life by buying the right clothes. The hours were long and she was on her feet for most of the day, but she enjoyed catering to the wealthy. Through them, she learned how to stand straight, talk softly, and walk gracefully.

Sarah couldn't believe her sister wanted to work. Patrick made enough to support all of them, and besides, respectable women never worked outside of the home. She couldn't imagine what Elizabeth was thinking.

Sarah planned to buy new clothes when she got to Chicago. Surprised to discover her brother's budget didn't include clothing for any of them, she thought of ways to skim money from the food budget. They didn't own a sewing machine; otherwise she could have sewed a new dress for herself. One day when she was out exploring the city, she walked through one of the department stores on State Street. She ran her hands over the smooth cotton dresses but was embarrassed to see the petticoats on public display. Sarah couldn't wait to be able to have some of those nice things. In Ireland, their necessities were purchased from cluttered dry-goods stores where merchants were unacquainted with modern times. In America, Sarah was wide-eyed and anxious to fit in. She wanted to dress like a city girl.

Sarah did all the cooking, cleaning, and shopping for the family. She accepted that, for she knew it wouldn't be long before she'd be married and out of the flat. She would argue with the clerks at the butcher shop, saying that ten cents a pound for pork chops was robbery. In Ireland she had butchered pigs and hung the carcasses in the hearth to smoke and sold the salted pork for a pittance.

Potatoes were thirty-nine cents a bushel, dried beans were nine cents a quart, and eggs were eighteen cents a dozen. Sarah purchased milk by the quart for six cents. Once in a while, she would put meat on the table, but only if she could get it for under a nickel per pound. Any money she could save by scrimping on groceries gave her more for herself. She wasn't about to be working like a servant in her brother's flat for nothing. Besides, it seemed only right, since Elizabeth wasn't doing her fair share.

Patrick cautioned her about buying milk that wasn't refrigerated because an outbreak of food poisoning had been reported. Other diseases such as smallpox, cholera, consumption, tuberculosis, and scarlet fever plagued the tenement buildings.

For the sake of her family's health, Sarah began to buy beer instead of milk. At least it was pasteurized and safer to drink. And if there was any left over at the end of the night, she drank it. That left more room in the icebox for other things. At least that's what she told Patrick.

CHAPTER 26

Michael Healy
Arrives in Chicago

November 1903

Michael Healy fidgeted with his cap as he looked out over the winter landscape. It was a tiring train ride, but sleep eluded him. He was anxious about his reunion with Sarah. She had written that Chicago had lots of jobs for anyone willing to work hard, and she was sure Michael would find something soon after arriving. She told him about Anne's rich husband and their lavish home. Michael detected envy in Sarah's words and worried that she expected a lifestyle as extravagant as her sister's. He answered her letter by telling her to be happy for Anne and suggested she visit her sister to re-kindle those old affections. Michael knew better than to tell Sarah what to do, but it made him unhappy to see her family members at odds with each other. It was bad enough that her brother Daniel was making a mess of his life.

Sarah's letter also said that her brother's fighting and his petty thieveries were enough to drive them crazy. They didn't know what to do about Daniel, and Patrick was too easy on him. Sarah was frightened that they would all be put on a ship and be sent back to Ireland. Her letters sounded so desperate that Michael decided he'd better get to Chicago before something terrible happened.

Michael's brother John wasn't able to see him off, but Maggie walked with him the six blocks through the streets of Bridgeport, Connecticut, arriving at the depot just minutes before the train departed. They barely had time to say a proper good-bye. Maybe that was good. Michael hated good-byes; he had already bid far too many farewells to people he loved. Thoughts of his mother evoked a terrible sadness within him, and when he closed his eyes, he could almost smell the musky odor from the peat that burned in the hearth inside her cottage.

Now, the steady rocking of the train helped relax him. Resting his head on the seat back, he thought of Maggie and their tearful good-bye at the station.

Jostled awake, Michael was surprised that he had slept. He noticed his cap was gone but soon found it under his shoes. While he brushed dirt off the top, he remembered the day his father gave it to him. It was a fine cap and had cost a month of rent money. It was his going away gift, his special remembrance of that day. Michael called it his good luck cap for the snug fit made him feel protected.

Thinking again of Maggie, Michael knew she was homesick for Ireland. Their brother John had taken to drinking in the saloons late into the night, leaving her to worry about her safety alone in the flat. Michael also worried about who would look after her when he was gone. He had asked her to come with him to Chicago, but she refused, saying there could be no living with Sarah. Maggie drew the line when it came to putting up with that "self-centered stubborn woman." Michael had hoped the two women would learn to like each other, but that never happened. Maggie told him, "I'd rather butcher pigs than spend a minute of my time in the same room with the likes of Sarah." He couldn't understand what there was about Sarah that made people so angry.

He was hungry and his body ached from sitting for so long. He asked the conductor when the train would arrive in Chicago. Checking his watch, the conductor said they'd arrive in less than two hours. Michael's empty stomach rumbled. Then, remembering the paper sack that Maggie had tucked into his pocket, he pulled it out and rejoiced when he saw the homemade bread spread with jam. He wolfed it down and felt better.

The scenery changed. Tall buildings and congested roads appeared suddenly, and Michael noticed the other passengers gathering up their coats. He ran his fingers through his thick blond hair, straightened his tie, buttoned his wool jacket, and got ready to get off the train.

The passengers moved forward when the train jerked to a halt and Michael joined the crowd headed for the depot. His legs were stiff, he was groggy, and he couldn't see much of anything because of the crowds. He found a safe place against a wall and waited for the depot to clear. He wasn't taking any chances of losing his suitcase or his money, for he had learned his lesson the hard way. One evening in Bridgeport as he headed to his flat after cashing his weekly check, someone hit him over the head and stole his money.

Sarah's letter said that he was to wait under the large clock over the ticket counter. He located the clock and waited. The crowd thinned, but no sign of Sarah. He was sure she knew the train schedule because he had mailed it to her and she promised to be there. One half hour went by and still, no sign of her. Most of the passengers and their families had already left the depot, and Michael began to worry that something awful had happened.

A voice from across the room startled him. "Michael," Sarah cried. They ran to each other and embraced. Sarah pulled back to look at him. Beginning at the top of his cap, she ran her eyes down to his scuffed boots. She told him how happy she was to see him and apologized for being late, for she had gotten into a fight with one of the neighbors. Before Michael could say how happy he was to see her, she was halfway through her story about the old biddy neighbor who hogged the clothesline.

When they passed through the depot doors, the odor of the city hit him. He couldn't believe the smell and the filth. Bridgeport wasn't the cleanest city, but it sparkled in comparison to Chicago. Here, he saw heaps of garbage, horse manure, and ashes dumped on the curbs, and the smoke that trailed from every chimney dusted the air with the coal residue. The biting November wind caught him off guard, and he quickly pulled his collar around his neck.

Patrick, Daniel, and Elizabeth welcomed their old friend into their flat. Sarah had prepared a feast. She spent the extra five cents a pound to buy pork chops. The potatoes were delicious and the parsnips were boiled to perfection. Patrick told Michael about their lives in Chicago and how difficult it was for the Irish to make a living. They were the last to be chosen for the good jobs. He suggested that Michael look to the police or the fire departments; he knew lots of Irish lads were getting hired in those places.

But, Michael had ideas of his own. He had heard about Chicago's vast transportation system and had his heart set on driving a trolley car. He had also read that good drivers were in demand. So although he had never driven a motor vehicle, he used to do a good job steering the horse cart in Ireland, and he was confidant that he could do just as well on the streets of Chicago.

Sarah announced that she and Michael would be married as soon as possible. She went on to tell everyone that she had spoken to Father O'Brien at the Holy Name Cathedral, and that they had set the date for December 6th. Looking over at Michael, she suggested they go to City Hall for their marriage license the very next day.

Lying on the floor in the Burns' front room that night, Michael wondered what his life would be like in Chicago. Sarah had a fire inside her soul, and he loved that about her. Sure, she could be tough, but then she had to be. She had grown up in one of the poorest cottages in Boyle. He remembered how his father would always provide fresh milk and salted pig to them. The entire town felt sorry for the five orphans. After their parents died, they had no one to look after them, and they barely scraped by. Michael vowed to be the best husband and to give her all the things in life she deserved.

Michael fell into a deep sleep, "the sleep of the demons," his mother used to say. When he was a boy, he awakened from those vivid dreams crying. They frightened him so, he thought they were real. That night his nightmares returned, and in them, he saw Sarah.

CHAPTER 27

Michael and Sarah Healy Chicago

1904-1907

A week before their marriage, Father O'Brien from Holy Name Cathedral approached Michael after Mass and asked where Sarah was. Michael was embarrassed. He hated to admit that Sarah seemed to have lost her faith. As children, they had attended St. Bridget's where they had their First Communions and Confirmations. All the families attended Mass there, for it was their Sunday obligation. Now, things were different with Sarah. When Michael questioned her, she reminded him of all her responsibilities. She complained about having to clean up after her brothers and sister, and who else was there to do the shopping and wash the clothes? Sunday mornings were the only time she could sleep late. Church was for those who didn't have all the things to do that she had. Michael told her she had a duty as a Catholic to her church, but Sarah wasn't about to be told what to do. And all that Father O'Brien could do was offer prayers for her in hopes that she would return to the fold.

Sarah was delighted to leave her brother's shabby flat. Michael located a small efficiency apartment at 915 N. Rush Street, not too far away from where the Burns' lived. Sarah had instructed Michael to be sure to find a place east of State Street because that was where the well-to-do people lived. Michael knew they couldn't afford the steep rents in that area, so he settled on a place in a fairly new building that was west of State Street. Sarah was already looking at expensive furniture and learning about the modern plumbing that was available to those who could afford it. Michael didn't mind as long as she was happy. He promised Sarah that one day she would have the fine home and lovely furnishings she wanted.

Shortly after their marriage, Michael secured a job driving an Omnibus. His supervisor assigned him to one of the least popular of the city's transportation modes—the horse carriage. Because of Michael's expertise in handling a horse cart, that job suited him well, and he was happy to have it. At least he was working.

Horse carts, pushcarts, the newly introduced automobile, and trolleys crowded the streets. Although the wooden bench was uncomfortable and the traffic frightening, Michael felt grand sitting on top of the coach. The Omnibus traveled around five miles per hour because of the congested streets. A conductor rode in the back and collected the nickel fares. Passengers entered through the rear of the coach, and when they wanted to exit, they pulled on a leather strap that was attached to Michael's leg. When Michael stopped the carriage, the conductor helped the passengers off. As horse-carriage and auto accidents increased, so, too, did pedestrian casualties.

Sarah placed some of Michael's weekly twelve-dollar paychecks into the bank and used the rest to pay their bills. The three dollars a week for rent included the cost of the coal. Three times each week, the driver of the coal wagon dumped large amounts of coal into the basement of each of the buildings on his route, leaving it up to the tenants to collect buckets full for their stoves.

They had to pay for their own ice, though, and it could be costly, depending on the weather. On cold days the ice lasted longer, and on hot humid days it began to melt before the deliveryman could get it into the cold storage box. Sarah continued to bargain shop for all their food, but one expense she considered necessary was the Schlitz beer that filled the tiny icebox. On hot days it cooled her, and on cold nights it warmed her.

Sarah looked in the shop windows and wished she could have the pretty dresses, feathered hats, and frilly petticoats that were displayed. She bought herself a few patterned housedresses and a new pair of shoes, but they weren't as pretty as the clothes in Field's windows. Michael and Sarah bought themselves heavy wool coats and hats, so they could keep warm and dry, but Sarah refused to leave her flat when the streets were snow-filled and icy unless she had boots. She had fallen a number of times and ruined her new shoes in the puddles and drifts. Fortunately, Michael's company issued uniforms. That savings allowed them to put a few more dollars in the bank every week. Sarah calculated how long it would be before they could have a big house and all the fine furnishings to fill it. One of her little schemes included delaying having children. The last thing she needed were more mouths to feed. She just wouldn't have it.

Michael couldn't understand why Sarah didn't respond to his affections at night when they settled into bed. He needed to be held and comforted; he was desperate for her love, but she pushed him away, telling him she was tired from all her hard work. He couldn't understand why she didn't wish to fulfill her marriage vows or why she seemed so cold.

One late afternoon after a hard day of work, Michael checked their mailbox before climbing the three flights of stairs to their flat and saw there was a letter. It was stuck in the back, and he wondered how long it had been there. The postmark read Bridgeport, Connecticut. What a wonderful surprise—a letter from his family! He had written to Maggie and John telling them of his marriage and his new life in Chicago, and had almost given up on receiving a reply. Taking two steps at a time, he rushed upstairs to share the news with Sarah.

When he opened the door to the flat, it was quiet inside and there were no potatoes simmering on the stove. Michael wondered where Sarah had gone. She was always home when he returned from work and always served him a hot meal. He couldn't wait for her, so he opened the letter. Reading each line carefully, his anticipation turned to sorrow and then to regret. Maggie had decided to return to Ireland. Their brother John had gotten worse. He drank up most of his wages, leaving little money for her to buy the things they needed. She missed their family in Ireland, and she worried about her father because he was now 101 years old. Maggie wrote that she would be better off at home on Carrowkeel. Michael looked at the date of the letter. It must have been sitting in their mailbox for over a week.

He had no opportunity to write back or travel to Bridgeport to bring her to Chicago. The news saddened him, and all alone in the tiny kitchen, he cried. He hadn't cried so hard since his mother died, nor had he thought much about Carrowkeel since arriving in America. Now, with Maggie gone, he realized how much he missed his family. For a moment he wondered if Sarah would consider returning to Ireland but then knew better than to suggest that to her. He had forgotten that Sarah didn't get along with any of his family.

Sarah arrived home soon after Michael. He could see from her many packages that she had been shopping. She pulled out a hat that had feathers sticking out from the sides and modeled it for him. Michael thought she looked like a bird. Sensing his disapproval, she removed the hat and busied herself with their supper.

Michael told Sarah about Maggie's decision to return to Ireland. Upset because he didn't admire her new hat, she ignored him and continued to peel the potatoes and carrots. Sarah expected him to be happy for her; Maggie had ruined it all with her letter.

1907

A new form of transportation arrived in Chicago and with it, a promotion for Michael. He was assigned to be a motorman on the electric streetcar. He was amazed at the overhead wire installed above the main streets. A long pole extending from the streetcar was attached to that wire. Michael had to learn how to reattach the pole because it very often fell from overhead, causing the car to stall and creating huge traffic jams.

Back at the Powerhouse, large steam engines turned the huge generators to produce the electricity needed to operate the streetcars. Michael was proud of his promotion and he served his passengers well. He was happy. It was easy for him to be happy at work. It was his home life that was troubling, but he went along with Sarah's wishes. He longed for children and hoped that one day Sarah would, too.

When summer arrived, Michael and Sarah spent weekends at the park listening to music. The Riverview Amusement Park was a big attraction, and they spent many Friday nights there, riding the roller coasters and eating cones of spun sugar candy. Some of the local saloons advertised themselves as family theaters, with music pavilions where vocal and instrumental entertainment was provided—the vaudeville stage. Engel's Opera Pavilion on Clark Street featured the music of a twelve-piece orchestra. It was all strictly high-tone—they advertised that "no ladies need blush" on their premises. Neighborhood theater groups staged performances at the Chicago Opera House, where Carrington, Holland, and Baby Olivette joined the Geraldine Sisters at Saturday matinees. It cost ten cents for the balcony and thirty cents for the main floor front and center seats.

Sarah loved the melodramas and kept track of her favorite performers through newspaper articles that followed their marriages, divorces, and deaths. She spent hours reading magazines and even gossiped a little with

Elizabeth, who she didn't see often, but enough to satisfy both of them.

Elizabeth had met and married a successful Chicago businessman. They purchased a lovely home on Burling Street on the north side. It was a three flat, which meant they could take in tenants and collect rent. Elizabeth's business experience at Marshall Field's prepared her well for managing their tenants.

Their brother Patrick worried continually about his brother and sisters. Daniel continued to break the law and drink himself into stupors. Anne, aside from being estranged from them, had lost a baby girl at birth, and Sarah hadn't visited any of them since she got married. Elizabeth failed to marry an Irishman, and he was not even a Catholic, for that matter. Patrick had thought the family could do better by leaving Ireland, but it seemed to have pulled them further apart. He felt he had failed his parents. He became depressed by the awful situation in America, for which he felt responsible.

Patrick asked his sisters to come to his flat on Madison Street for a family conference. He had something to discuss. Anne made the excuse she had to look after her sickly neighbor; Sarah was too busy taking care of Michael, and Elizabeth's husband refused to go with her. So, it was left to Patrick to decide what to do about Daniel. He would take him back to Ireland, back to the cottage on Ardmoyle where their lives would surely be better. It was easy, for there was nothing to sell, nothing to pack, nor was there anyone to say good-bye to.

Only Elizabeth met her brothers at the depot on the day they left. They cried and promised to see each other again someday, but Elizabeth knew as she watched her brothers leave that she might never see them again. Daniel was stooped and seemed older than his thirty-one years, and Patrick, at the age of twenty-seven, walked as if he had a great weight on his shoulders. Elizabeth hoped they would find happiness and for just a moment wished she could go back with them. With a heavy heart she walked away from the depot, and for the second time in her life, Elizabeth felt alone and abandoned.

CHAPTER 28

The Webs We Weave

1909-1929

She couldn't help herself. His embrace had been warm and his touch soothed her nerves on that particular night when his desires had awakened hers. She had been so careful not to let that happen, and now she had to tell him. At first, she didn't believe it could be true, but she hadn't been feeling good. When she couldn't keep her breakfast down, she knew.

Sarah wasn't looking forward to telling Michael. Not now! Not before she had her house. She spent the entire day sulking and blaming her husband for her lot in life.

Michael rejoiced at the news that Sarah was pregnant. Finally, they would have the family he wanted. He wasn't worried that she was angry now, for he knew in his heart that she would be a good mother when the time came. He watched her from across the room and his heart ached. To hold her or to comfort her in any way was something he wouldn't dare; she had her boundaries, and he knew not to cross them.

Michael took extra care to make sure she stayed off her feet. He bought the groceries on the way home from work and hung the clothes on the back porch line so she wouldn't have to bother with the nosey neighbors. He hauled up buckets of coal and insisted she stay close to the stove, and if she didn't feel like cooking that was fine with him. Michael didn't mind spoiling her, for soon they would have a baby. He couldn't wait to write to Maggie to tell her the good news.

The pregnancy went well, as expected, except for Sarah's constant complaining. Every night she cried to Michael and blamed him for having to put her dreams aside. When life stirred inside her, she ignored the sensation and refused to accept what was happening.

The parish priest visited and asked her to return to the church. He offered to pray the rosary with her, but she would have none of it. Crying to him, she asked where he had been when she didn't have warm boots or when she needed someone to help carry up the coal. She asked if the priest would be buying her the house she wanted, and would he be there at night when the baby was sick and required tending? Sarah took that opportunity to vent her anger on the priest who came only to comfort her and try to save her soul. He surely wouldn't make that mistake again!

Sarah gave birth to a beautiful baby girl and named her Mary, after her mother. Michael's life changed the moment he held his new daughter. He promised Mary the world and all the happiness in it. The baby resembled his sister Maggie, and that caused him to dance the Irish jig around the kitchen while holding Mary in his arms.

He hadn't heard from his family in Ireland yet and was delighted to receive the long awaited letter. Maggie wrote that their father had died six months ago at the age of 104. She went on to tell Michael about the largest funeral ever in Boyle, with over one hundred neighbors in attendance. The funeral procession traveled from their cottage on Carrowkeel to Killarght Graveyard.

Tears came easily for Michael. The cap that he treasured, the gift from his father on the day he left their cottage for America, lay folded on the table. He picked it up and held it to his face so that his crying wouldn't wake the baby.

Sarah watched Michael from across the room. She couldn't help feeling sorry for him but had no idea how to comfort him. Her only thoughts were that Michael's father was an old man and had lived far too long. Did he expect his father to live forever?

Wiping his face on his sleeve, Michael continued reading the letter. Maggie said she'd given birth to a baby boy last year. She wasn't married, and the baby's father had left for America soon after learning Maggie was pregnant. Michael could barely catch his breath for the pain that pierced his heart. Not only was his father gone but also his sister was hurting. She had given birth to an illegitimate child, the son of a no-good McCarthy man. Michael remembered the man and couldn't believe that Maggie would have fallen for his empty promises. Michael knew only too well what happened to unmarried Irish girls who found themselves pregnant. But he also knew that his father and his brother would never banish Maggie to a convent laundry, nor would they have given the child away. Maggie's words assured Michael that she was doing well despite the gossip and emotional pain she had to endure in Boyle. The priest at St. Bridget's agreed to baptize Maggie's son, Johnny, but only during a private ceremony and without posting it in the church newsletter. She ended her letter by saying she was happy that Michael was the father of a beautiful baby girl.

Sarah picked up the letter from the table where Michael had dropped it. She commented that it was no surprise to her that Maggie had gotten herself pregnant and said Maggie should be ashamed of herself and do the right thing by giving the baby to another family to raise. Michael stood up with such force that the chair in which he sat hit the wall behind him, sending pictures crashing to the floor. Michael raised his hand to her and Sarah backed away, fearing him for the very first time in their lives. Never had he raised his voice or a hand to her, but she realized she had gone too far this time. Awakened by the commotion, baby Mary began to cry.

Michael never really understood why his family, as well as some of the neighbors, avoided Sarah, why she had no friends or why the butcher and the street vendors turned their backs to her. He knew she had spirit and believed she was capable of being a good wife. Those who knew Michael felt sorry for him but could offer little advice, and Michael didn't welcome it, nor did he see what everyone else saw when they got to know Sarah. Even now, as easy as it was for him to see, first hand, the true Sarah, he forgave her the minute he realized what he had almost done.

1912

On days when the summer sun warmed the grass, Michael and Sarah wheeled the baby to Lincoln Park. They visited the zoo and, sometimes, they visited Sarah's sisters, even though the visits were never very pleasant. Anne had a baby boy named William, and Elizabeth had a son called Sylvester, Jr.

That winter, Sarah was particularly miserable. Her feet swelled and she couldn't fit into any of her clothes. Michael knew something was wrong, but he had learned to stay away when things weren't going well for her. Their relationship had been strained since Maggie's letter, but somewhere in the back of his mind, Michael still carried the belief that Sarah would change once she had her house. When he heard that she was pregnant again, he was overjoyed. But now, there would be no peace in their tiny flat.

Sarah gave birth to another baby girl on September 16. Michael beamed; a little girl they called Ellen after his mother. The nurse misunderstood when Sarah said the baby's name, and she recorded it as Helen. To avoid confrontation, Michael said nothing; lately, Sarah was worse than ever and prone to fits of anger and rage. Now, finally, she had begun to frighten him.

1914-1915

Michael couldn't wait to tell Sarah about the house he found for them on Orchard Street. Taking the stairs two at a time, he arrived breathless in their kitchen. Sarah didn't pay any attention to him; she was busy tending their two toddlers and cooking supper. He rattled on about how close it was to the streetcar barn on Clark Street, and it was just one block over from Elizabeth's house, and then he told her he purchased it.

Sarah cried from happiness. The two little girls, not understanding, ran to their father, for it was with him they felt safe.

Sarah couldn't wait to leave the ugly tenement flat. Finally, she was getting the life she deserved. She had saved enough money to buy not only the house but also the furniture and other necessities. Michael hoped and prayed that moving into the new house would be the event that made a difference in their lives.

When moving day arrived, they piled their dishes, pots, furniture, and clothing on the curb and waited for the horse cart. Sarah dressed the children in their best outfits and insisted Michael wear his suit, for it was important they make a good impression.

Sarah spent hours polishing the beautiful wood-inlaid furniture. Her home was a showcase, with large comfortable chairs in the living room and a solid mahogany-dining ensemble in the adjoining room. The large kitchen had a new stove, an icebox, and an iron sink with a faucet. The house had a flush toilet and a coal furnace in the basement that not only heated the house but also the water pipes. There were two bedrooms. Michael and Sarah slept in the room off the dining room, while the girls shared the small room off the kitchen. Upstairs was a small apartment that Sarah planned to rent out. The extra income would give her enough money to buy the fur coat she had seen in the window of Marshall Field's on State Street. Sarah had never been happier, and Michael was relieved to finally have peace in the family.

1916

Sarah collected thirty dollars a month from the upstairs apartment. The young couple who rented it had a three-year-old son who occasionally came down to play with the Healy girls. Sarah didn't mind because it kept the girls busy, but she didn't encourage friendship with her tenants; she didn't want anyone to know anything about her business. Sarah had all she could do to keep away from the prying eyes of the neighbors. She didn't wish to reveal anything about her personal life with Michael. She had thick wooden blinds installed on every window, and she covered them with heavy draperies made from beautifully colored and patterned imported fabric. She was sure the nosey neighbors wanted to peek inside her windows to see what she had.

Their white clapboard house had a large elevated front porch fifteen steps up from the front yard. From the porch, Sarah had a clear view of the neighbors' porches on either side of her. She sat for hours every day, hidden by the thick wooden slats of the porch railing, watching the comings and goings of the neighbors. She insisted that Michael walk down the alley and enter their back door after work because she feared he might have conversations with the neighbors and tell them about how poor they had been in Ireland.

On the night of St. Patrick's Day, Sarah's sisters and their families joined them in celebration of the holiday. The women cooked all week in preparation for the feast, and Michael looked forward to the merriment, for it was one of the few times during the year that Sarah was remotely civil to him. The drinking began shortly after the children were put to bed and lasted well into the night. Long after her sisters and their families had gone home, Sarah and Michael stayed up to finish the beer that was left. Since they had their telephone installed, they were able to call the liquor store and have their beer brought to their back door.

Sarah seemed to have everything any woman would want or need to be happy. From all appearances, the Healy family seemed to be enjoying the good life. Inside was hidden another story. Sarah's short temper and her inability to deal with the smallest problem made Michael's life a living hell, but Michael still felt responsible for Sarah's happiness.

The month of June found Sarah more hostile than usual. None of her clothes fit and she suspected she was pregnant again. She thought back to March and to St. Patrick's night and could barely remember the event, but now she was angry with herself for not being more careful when she gave in to Michael's desires. She approached him with the news of a baby.

The routine in Michael's life suited him. He was respected in his position as motorman for the Chicago Surface Lines and managed to hold on to one of the most coveted routes—the #22 Clark Street run. He was a Cubs baseball fan and especially liked driving by Federal Field during a game; he enjoyed the crowds and all the activity that surrounded the ball field on the corner of Clark and Addison. And his two little girls meant the world to him. He thought Sarah ran the house efficiently; she kept the children clean and well fed and, for the most part, did a good job in providing the necessities within the household budget. After thirteen years with her, this was all he had come to expect. When he heard she was having another baby, he was overjoyed, though he had to be careful in his response. He knew how she felt about being pregnant.

On December 16th, a son was born to them and was named John, after Sarah's father. Michael noticed a difference in his wife. It was as though she had been waiting for a boy all this time. She fussed over and cared for John and readily awoke during the night for the feedings. Michael knew better than to question her. He was simply happy that she had adjusted so well to the new baby.

On hot summer nights, Michael and Sarah walked their little ones to Lincoln Park and spent the night under the stars. Those were wonderful times when neighbors and friends gathered to enjoy the beautiful lakefront with its gentle breezes. All the families shared food while the children romped way past their bedtime, but it was okay because the park provided them an all-night playground. On these nights, Sarah relaxed and almost forgot how much she mistrusted everyone.

1917-1920

Michael discussed the idea of becoming United States citizens. Sarah encouraged it, for she had been living in constant fear of being sent back to Ireland. It would be over her dead body that she would return to the poverty and hopelessness in that God-forsaken place. Michael filed his Declaration of Intent on April 10, 1917, and the petition was finally accepted on January 13, 1920. They hung the flag they received during the ceremony at the courthouse over their front door.

Sarah knew Prohibition was coming. The owner of the neighborhood liquor store had informed his best customers of it. The upcoming Eighteenth Amendment to the Constitution would ban the sale of intoxicating beverages.

Sarah couldn't believe the impact this was having on her life. Her weekends seemed unusually long, and the absence of beer in the house just didn't set well with her. She heard about people who were brewing their own beer and hiding it. Sarah investigated the purchase of equipment required for home brewing and discovered she could buy those items at the Woolworth's dime store on Clark Street. Her neighbors must have had the same idea because empty bottles became scarce. She purchased Stroh's Hopped Malt Syrup which, according to the label, was supposed to be used for baking. She hoarded all the necessary supplies and put Michael to work mixing it up. Unfortunately, the brew tasted awful, but it provided the Saturday night enjoyment Sarah had come to rely on. Michael didn't like breaking the law, but Sarah considered herself above the law. And now that she was a citizen, she believed her rights were guaranteed. Besides, almost everyone was involved in home brewing. Michael buried the bottles of beer in the back yard late at night just in case the police came knocking on their door.

Sarah decided to add to their income by taking in a border, someone to live in their home. Since they had only two small bedrooms, she could barely accommodate the twenty-two year old mechanic named Clinton Bougham. Michael argued against bringing in a stranger to sleep in their living room. He couldn't believe that she was willing to risk the comfort and safety of the family for a few extra dollars. But as always, Michael gave in, for he knew better than to cross her.

Automobiles were becoming popular, and Clinton introduced Sarah and Michael to his sporty new 1924 Packard. Sarah told Michael that she had to have a car and insisted their daughters Mary and Helen learn to drive so they could take her shopping. The girls, of course, were delighted, happy to drive their mother wherever she wanted to go. Helen, at the age of twelve, learned to drive the new Ford through the pedestrian traffic and the horse-drawn carriages of the busy city. Michael was happy to see Sarah take an interest in something concerning the family; he could see that the automobile had been a good idea and thanked Clinton for the wonderful suggestion.

Everyone envied them. They had a beautiful home, fine furnishings, three beautiful, well-behaved children, and a new car—they had it all! Sarah felt like a queen. She was happy for the life she was convinced she deserved.

Clinton knew about the home brewing; in fact, he helped Michael fill the bottles and bury them. He didn't mind helping, since he also enjoyed the brew after a hard day's work. And when Michael went off to bed early, Clinton enjoyed Sarah's company. He had a good thing and became comfortable living in the Healy home—too comfortable. He was to be called Sarah's nephew, in case anyone asked.

It was the "Roaring Twenties" and Sarah was becoming a modern woman. She bobbed her hair, bought fashionable short skirts and even smoked cigarettes. She applied lipstick and rouge. She purchased Life Magazine, which showcased flappers dancing the Charleston and the Blackbottom. Ladies were being arrested at the beaches for appearing in the new one-piece bathing suits. Rudy Vallee crooned while Paul Whiteman's jazz band provided them with toe-tapping rhythms over the wireless radios. The economy was booming, and the Healy family had the money to participate in the good times. Sarah and Michael lived the elegant life formerly available only to the rich.

Sarah became a secretive drinker, darting savage glances toward anyone who came within ten feet of her. She positioned herself in the far corner of the living room, and when night fell, the only illumination was the streak of moonlight that found its way through the thick slatted blinds. Under the influence of alcohol, Sarah banished discretion and somewhere in all of this, she found herself pregnant. Michael knew the baby wasn't his. Even more disastrous, their daughter Mary, sixteen, was also pregnant and Clinton was the only possible culprit.

Michael's world came crashing down. How had he not seen the signs? He could say nothing to Sarah because he still feared her. His beautiful daughter Mary, the victim of a negligent mother, was paying for Sarah's sins, and for once in his life, Michael felt defeated.

Sarah hid her little secret and went about her business as if nothing had happened, but hated Mary for revealing her as an unfit mother. Mary's condition was not acceptable, though Sarah considered hers perfectly all right. How dare her daughter bring shame to their family!

Michael felt powerless to do anything. The night he discovered the pregnancies, he confronted Clinton, who denied having anything to do with their situations and threatened to turn Michael into the authorities for home brewing. Michael was terrified to think that he could lose everything. So he did what he thought was best—he did nothing.

He sat in the large kitchen. Steam hissed from the radiator; the distant sound of children's laughter could be heard from outside back porch windows. Water from the potatoes boiled over, causing the fire to spit and crackle. Helen ran into the room, removed the pot, and carried it to the sink; she drained the potatoes and set the pot to soak. She ached for her father and felt despair for her family. There was nothing she could do or say to ease the pain. She felt helpless.

Helen was Michael's only happiness. John was a good boy, but because Sarah favored him, he had become her loyal child, and Michael had no comfort from him. Helen was a wonderful daughter: kind, considerate, and willing to do whatever was asked of her. She never complained. Michael saw traces of Maggie in her face and her manner, and he thanked the saints in heaven for giving him the one thing in his life that would always be true. He had taught Helen the Irish songs that called to mind his youth in Ireland. And with a wee bit of home brew, he was content for at least the evening.

1926

Sarah gave birth to a baby boy and named him Lawrence. Michael had no idea why the baby would be given such a name, but it didn't matter, and he never asked. Mary went into labor two months later. She lay on the bed in her tiny bedroom off the kitchen, and with each labor pain came the added humiliation of her mother's strap. The edge of the leather belt caught Mary's flesh and blood trickled onto the sheets. This terrified Mary even more, for she thought she would surely die. Helen cowered behind the door, unable to believe her mother's cruelty, but Sarah was so involved in administering the beating that she never even noticed Helen in the room. When the baby came, Sarah put the little bundle next to her own son in the cradle next to the radiator.

The next morning, a young couple arrived in a shiny Dodge Touring Car with side curtains and a driver. Sarah handed over Mary's newborn son to the strangers at the door. Before taking the baby from Mary, Sarah told her, "I'm about to teach you the lesson of your life."

Sarah wasn't quite through. One week later, Mary was put in the hospital and forced to undergo a hysterectomy. There would be no more babies for Mary—her mother made sure of that.

The baby Lawrence was guaranteed a place in the family, and Sarah went about her life as if nothing untoward had happened. Michael couldn't blame the child for the sins of his mother, and he accepted the baby as his own. He was baptized Lawrence Healy, and would grow up to become Sarah's favorite child.

Michael couldn't leave. Where would he go? To return to Ireland would bring his pain and humiliation to the family there. They had never liked Sarah, and he wasn't about to run to them with details of the most recent catastrophe. He had stopped writing to Maggie and, sadly, had put that chapter of his life behind him.

Mary quit school and began to drink. She stayed out all night with boys who hung out around the schoolyard. Sarah didn't seem to care about her anymore, and Michael no longer felt any compassion. He'd hear Mary staggering through the front door. Too drunk to find the living room door, she often spent the entire night on the floor of the front hall. He saw his daughter's steely eyes watching Sarah as she tended to her baby. Michael knew that Mary hated everyone in the house, but worst of all, she hated herself more.

Michael lived in a house of strangers. They passed each other in the hallway, sat at the same dinner table, and together listened to the radio in the living room filled with all its fine furnishings.

Michael never asked Sarah who the father of Lawrence was, nor did he ever talk with Mary about the horror she had survived. He stopped speaking to both of them. The routine of his job, the simple pleasures of a home brew and spending time with his darling Helen, were all a man was entitled to. At least, that's what he told himself.

Grandparents
Married: December 6, 1903

MICHAEL HEALY

Born: June 10, 1879
          Townland of Carrowkeel
          Boyle, County
            Roscommon, Ireland

Emigrated: July 22, 1903
Departed: Queenstown, Ireland
Arrived: Ellis Island, New York
Resided: Connecticut and Illinois
Died: August 1, 1950

SARAH BEIRNE

Born: August 4, 1881
          Townland of Ardmoyle
          Boyle, County
            Roscommon, Ireland

Emigrated: July 22, 1903
Departed: Queenstown, Ireland
Arrived: Ellis Island, New York
Resided: Illinois
Died: July 30, 1966

Helen Healy at her parents' home on Orchard Street Chicago, Illinois   1933

Sarah Healy with her new car   1930s

CHAPTER 29

Mike Carberry Shea in Chicago's Packingtown

1929-1935

Mike Shea, Bridget's youngest son, knew the smell. He had grown up with it in Omaha. Sometimes it seemed kind of sweet, and he could almost taste it, and other times it was rancid. It was a little different every day but was always there with its lingering presence. Mike's workplace consisted of mud, railroad tracks, cattle cars, cattle pens, overhead runways, great ugly brick buildings, men on ponies, raucous grunts and squeals, and nauseating odors. Fortunately, he had been able to secure a job in the office, but most times he supervised the yard.

Standing in mud up to his ankles, Mike watched as the stream of enormous hogs pushed themselves into the overcrowded pens. He knew they were nervous because they smelled danger, or perhaps they were merely skittish from hearing the cries of the other animals.

Mike witnessed their execution. It was he who helped direct them into their pens, commanded the men to attach the heavy chains to their hind legs; it was he who accompanied them to the waiting butcher. He was fascinated by the way pigs reacted to their impending death. Some of them came in squealing; others were silent. Some in their distress pressed against each other. Others merely waited in resignation with bowed heads.

This was not a job for the faint of heart. Without prejudice or pity, Mike recorded the number of boxcars as they emptied. He accounted for more than four thousand hogs and two thousand steers a week.

His job as a supervisor was an important one. His experience as a stockyard clerk in Omaha had guaranteed him a good job in the Chicago yards, and although the work was dirty, he performed beyond expectations. He was respected in his circle of managers, but he became a target for abuse from union organizers. The laborers who worked under him didn't trust him because he didn't support their labor movement. Mike was careful to watch his back. He knew that an "accident" could easily be covered up in the hog pens.

Forty cents an hour gave him an annual wage of twelve hundred dollars. Mike lived comfortably enough in a rented flat that provided running water and a flush toilet down the hall for ten dollars a week. Mike wasn't fussy. He came from poor. To him, a warm place with a bed and a comfortable chair was all he needed.

Marriage was the last thing on his mind. He couldn't even imagine what it would take to meet someone. He was shy and, working ten hours a day, six days a week, he didn't have much free time. None of the girls who worked in the pickling room among the rows of enormous hogs heads appealed to him. Not one of the hundreds of young women he trained to poke cords through the hams in the smokehouse caught his eye. And, of course, any girl he courted would have to be Irish!

Mike thought a lot about his mother. In fact, not a day went by that he didn't wonder how his life would have been had she lived. He would never have left Omaha. Cecelia had written to him about their father's death, but he couldn't go back home to be near his family—not with the memories of his mother always so painful. After work, alone in his flat, Mike was happy to pour his scotch and spend the evening drinking those painful memories away.

Mike continued to stay away from his family in Omaha but kept in touch with his sister Cecelia, who lived in Kansas with her family. They had always been close, and he missed her. Thinking it was time for a vacation, Mike took a week off to travel to Kansas. On the train, he thought about the bicycle he was taking to Cecelia's children. He'd seen the shiny red Schwinn in a store window on 47th and Ashland, just three blocks from where he worked, and he couldn't wait for them to see it. He knew they would love it.

It surprised him to realize Cecelia had seven children, with another on the way, and he was embarrassed to have brought only one bicycle. Not only that, he had bought a boy's bike, and there was only one son big enough to ride it. The four girls, however, waited their turn, happy for any bike, even if they had to share it. Mike was charmed by Cecelia's children, and sometime during the visit, he decided it was time for him to find a wife and settle down.

Back in Chicago, he yearned for companionship. Things were hard during the Depression, and many people didn't have enough money to afford much of anything, but Mike had a good job with a secure future, and he wanted someone to share it with. The silence of his small flat reminded him of how lonely he was.

One hot summer evening, walking through his neighborhood, he noticed a large crowd at the end of the block and decided to see what was so interesting. An Irish saloon was hosting a block party, and he was invited to join the festivities. He did, and he ended up having a few too many drinks. He was having difficulty following conversations. Leaning over in an attempt to get off the bar stool, he heard a popping sound and felt a burning sensation in his leg. When he stood, he fell to the floor and passed out from the pain.

The next thing he knew, he was in a hospital being attended to by a lovely nurse. For a moment he thought he had died and gone to heaven. He asked her if she was an angel. Propped up in his hospital bed, Mike welcomed a few visitors from the plant and learned what happened in the bar that night. Disputes between labor and management were becoming more numerous and dangerous. Tensions were thick in the saloon on that night, and when a drunken laborer recognized Mike at the bar, he aimed a gun at his chest and fired. Luckily, someone shoved the gunman's arm, and it discharged as it hit the floor. The bullet flew to Mike's right leg and shattered part of the shinbone. He would be laid up for several weeks, but he didn't mind; he was alive and falling in love with his nurse.

He watched as she tugged at the gauze on his leg, gently removing the bandage. Mike admired her long, slender fingers and honey gold hair. Wisps of curls escaped her bun and hung in ringlets on her smooth neck. Her shoulders were strong. Mike was sure she came from a good Irish family. And when she looked at him with her big blue eyes, he felt faint. Kathleen O'Leary was a good nurse and he was sure his mother would have been happy for him to have a wife as pretty as she.

He asked for some paper and a pencil, telling her he wanted to write to his family. But that wasn't true; Mike never told his family in Omaha or Cecelia about that night in the saloon. He wanted the writing materials so he could write a poem to Kathleen. Having had no experience with women, other than his mother and sisters, Mike thought that if he loved Kathleen, she would love him, too.

After three weeks, Mike was able to stand and walk without a cane, and the doctor told him he could return to work. The time was right. Confident that Kathleen would return his affections, he presented his poem to her, heartfelt words beautifully written on a wrinkled, stained sheet of paper. Kathleen read every word seriously and with great interest. Mike could hardly wait for her response.

Unprepared and shocked by his feelings for her, Kathleen told him that she was in love with someone else. Mike was devastated. How could he have made such a mistake? He was angry with himself and with the nurse who, he felt, had led him to believe that she loved him.

Mike had not received a paycheck while he was in the hospital, and he sold the poem to pay the hospital bill. The poem was titled *Have You Ever Been Lonely, Have You Ever Been Blue* and was bought by someone who put a melody to it. Whenever Mike heard that song, he had to leave the room because it reminded him of the woman he loved who never loved him back.

Although Mike showed up for work every day, he was listless and no longer cared. He wasn't eating the right food, nor was he getting a good night's sleep. In his dreams he saw shadowy images of Kathleen mixed with clouded visions of his mother. Their dreamy whispers convinced Mike that Kathleen *was* Bridget, returned to him.

The slaughter of all those animals was getting hard for him take. There had been a time when working in the stockyards made it easy for him to hide his emotions. He had not felt uncomfortable with so much death around him. Now, at the age of thirty-seven and with his life half over, he knew that to survive he had to find someone to love and love him in return.

CHAPTER 30

Helen Healy Leaves Orchard Street

1934-1937

At twenty-two, Helen was ready to begin life on her own. It was time to put the horrors of life with her mother behind her. She felt sorry for Mary; she knew their mother had destroyed any hope of her happiness. Helen was going to make sure that didn't happen to her.

She would miss her father. Although he was a physical presence in the house, his spirit had left him years ago. It was obvious that he was merely going through the motions of his existence. Every day he got up early for work, came home in time for supper, and listened to the radio before going to bed. Sundays were hell because he had nowhere to go.

An uncle, Mr. Bonds, had passed away and left Helen a sizeable amount of money in his will, enough to buy an automobile and to live independently for a couple of years. Helen purchased a shiny new black Packard for the price of one thousand dollars. The sleek coupe was almost as long as the streetcar her father drove, at least, she thought it might be. The eight-cylinder, three-speed vehicle was the perfect car for her.

With her bags packed and stashed in the trunk, she bade farewell to Orchard Street and all of its terrible memories and drove toward Route 66—the most direct way to California.

She drove on paved as well as unpaved roads. The highway was rough in places, but the Packard performed magnificently. With each bump and rut, Helen bounced and swayed to the tunes of The Benny Goodman Orchestra that crackled from the radio. She drove fearlessly through small towns. When she stopped for gas, the attendants peeked inside the car windows, searching for her husband. And when she stopped for the night, hotel desk clerks looked for the spouse they expected would be traveling with her. Helen drove through the hot, dry plains of Oklahoma, the dust bowl of Texas, cactus-filled Arizona, the foothills of New Mexico, and finally into the rugged mountainous region of Southern California.

During the long drive, she thought about her father, her sister, and her conniving brothers, John and Lawrence, who were already involved with the criminals of the neighborhood. Helen's father had caught John with a box of expensive jewelry. John told him he found it on the street and that he planned to sell the pieces. John's goal was to own his own tavern. That didn't surprise Helen; she knew that drinking was the family's honored and favorite pastime. Her father was powerless, and her mother had failed to provide the stability, compassion, and love that would have made a difference in all of their lives. Helen was sure that other families lived differently than theirs. She planned on driving as far away as possible from the demons on Orchard Street, and with each hundred miles logged, her determination to find the good life was strengthened.

A week later, she arrived in Buckman Springs, California and made an inquiry at a coffee shop about a place to stay. She was told to contact Betty McGee, a recent widow, and given directions to the small farm just up the road. Not even taking time to eat, Helen drove directly to the farmhouse. She was tired and hoped to be settled before dark.

The meeting between the two women went well, and Betty suggested an arrangement. Helen would drive her into town to purchase supplies whenever necessary. And in exchange, Helen would receive room and board. They agreed it was a perfect situation for both of them.

Helen was given the larger bedroom that offered a clear view of the mountains. White lace curtains draped the large paned windows. The walls were papered in tiny lavender flowers, and the sturdy wood furniture was polished to a high gloss. The thick mattress, covered with fluffy feather quilts, looked inviting, and Helen couldn't wait for her first good night's sleep in over a week.

A friendship developed. The women enjoyed each other's company. Helen was delighted to have found such a safe and lovely place. The farmhouse backed up to an orange grove whose sweet lingering scent permeated the dry air. Helen wrote to her father to tell him that she had found paradise.

Betty was curious about why Helen never talked about her family. She knew only that Helen had traveled from

Chicago and suspected there was a secret locked up inside of her. In the evening, when they sat on the porch enjoying the cloudless night sky, Betty shared stories of her wonderful husband, who died from a heart attack. She told Helen how she would never get over losing the only man she had ever loved. Helen couldn't imagine what that must feel like, and she envied that special relationship.

They drove into town early one July morning and filled the car with tools and garden supplies. Afterwards, they stopped at a restaurant for lunch. Over coffee and shared stories, they giggled like schoolgirls.

A handsome young man seated at the counter sipped his mug of coffee and strained to hear their conversation. He didn't mean to eavesdrop, but there was something about the young woman that struck him. He liked the pretty flowered sundress she wore, and he admired her wavy brown hair that was pulled away from her face with barrettes. From across the room he noticed how her blue eyes sparkled when she turned toward the sun. It was obvious that she was new in town. She seemed to have a "city" look about her—and besides, he'd never seen her before.

When the women settled their bill and got up to leave, he seized the opportunity and made it to the door before they did. Nonchalantly, he pulled it open, and in a royal gesture ushered them out. Flattered, they thanked him and proceeded to the car.

He recognized Betty, but she didn't remember him. His father had done odd jobs around their farm, and he used to go along to help during the summers. Thinking that would provide the perfect excuse, later that day he saddled his horse and rode out to the farm to see if they needed any help.

Helen saw someone approaching on horseback. She placed her pan of green beans next to the porch swing and walked into the yard to investigate. He jumped down from his horse and introduced himself. His crystal blue eyes hypnotized Helen, and when he removed his cowboy hat, she admired his thick curly brown hair. Her curiosity piqued, she invited him in for a glass of lemonade.

It was a lovely few hours. The man named Bill was not only charming but also intelligent. He told Helen and Betty about his ranch five miles down the road and about how he had inherited it from his father, who had recently passed away. He lived alone and made his living by working bit parts in Hollywood films. The ladies were fascinated with him and his stories about the actors and actresses. When he got up to leave, Betty invited him to have dinner with them the next night.

Helen and Bill liked each other immediately and found it easy to talk to one another. They soon became inseparable. He wanted children, she wanted children; he loved living in California and she loved it as well. He called her Sunny because she brightened his life. Within three months, they were making plans for their wedding.

Helen was never happier. All the good things she had ever dreamed of were coming true. Every Sunday, Bill picked her up for early Mass, and afterwards, they went to the coffee shop for breakfast. They lingered there for hours, planning their future. Helen thought her life couldn't get any better.

Late one October evening, sitting under a sky crowded with stars, Helen and Betty discussed the wedding and whether or not Helen would be inviting her family. Helen was sure her mother wouldn't come. Besides, just thinking about Sarah caused Helen's stomach to knot. No, she wouldn't be inviting her mother. But she wanted her father to come and promised herself that she would call him in the morning. Observing the twinkling constellations overhead, Helen made a wish on a falling star that she would be as happy for the rest of her life as she was at that moment.

The phone call came in the middle of the night. There had been an accident, and could she come immediately. Helen and Betty drove to the San Diego Hospital, where they were directed to the emergency room.

On his way home from work, Bill's car had gone off the road and down an embankment. He had been asking for her all night. She rushed into his room. The look on the doctor's face told Helen what she didn't want to hear, and she clasped her hands over her ears. She hadn't arrived in time. He died a few minutes before she got there.

Helen closed her suitcase. It had taken hours to pack all the things she wanted to take with her—all the memories of her life in California, the only place she had ever been happy. After saying good-bye to Betty, she got in the car and headed for Route 66.

During the long drive back to Chicago, she cried, beat the steering wheel, and screamed at God. Her heart was broken; she was broken. Not sure what to do after Bill died, she thought it best to leave the painful memories and return to her father. She knew he needed her and, although she couldn't move back into her mother's house, she would live close enough to visit her father on Sundays.

When she arrived in Chicago, Helen noticed the dark clouds that had descended over the city. She wasn't looking forward to seeing her mother. Her plan was to stop for only a short visit and then be on her way. She had a friend, who lived near the stockyards, and she could stay with her while she sorted out her life.

Sitting across the table from her mother, Helen felt obligated to tell Sarah how happy she had been with Bill and how much they had loved each other. As expected, her mother was glib and smug about the news of Bill's death. Helen knew that Sarah couldn't stomach any of her children being happier than she, and since her mother wasn't happy, no one else had a right to be. Just then, the back doorbell rang and Sarah rushed to answer it. She returned with two quart bottles of Blatz beer. Helen knew only too well what the evening would bring: her mother would drink, Mary would go out early and return home late with a strange man she had picked up in a bar, John and Lawrence would leave to meet their hoodlum friends, and her father would retire early to bed. Helen glimpsed Clinton sitting in the darkest corner of the dining room. Sarah poured a large glass of beer and took it over to him.

When Sarah returned to the kitchen, Helen was gone.

*Helen Healy on her way to
Buckman Springs,
California   1934*

Helen Healy with her friend Betty McGee in Buckman Springs   1935

CHAPTER 31

Helen and Mike

1937

S
he noticed him watching her but thought nothing
of it. He was a regular in the coffee shop and
never really spoke with anyone. She guessed he
worked at the stockyards because he arrived for lunch at
the same time as the other men who worked in the yards.
What interested her was his suit and tie, and his shoes were
always polished. He wasn't a laborer—that was obvious.
Today, though, he didn't look well; his face was pale and
his suit looked too big. She asked her boss if he knew who
he was, and all he could say was that his name was Mike
Shea.

Helen was a cashier in the busy coffee shop located
around the corner from the stockyards. It was only a few
blocks from where she lived, temporarily, in her friend
Jean's apartment. Helen didn't need the money because she
still had some of her inheritance, but she thought it would
be good for her to have something to do, something other
than missing Bill. At night in her dreams, she saw them
happily married and living at the beautiful ranch surrounded by mountains. She knew she should go to church

and pray for his soul, but she couldn't; she was still angry. If only she had driven faster to the hospital, or if only she had reached all the green lights before they turned red. If only.... The second-guessing drove her crazy, and there were times when she didn't think she would make it through the day. The cashier job was a lifesaver; it provided the necessary distraction.

Jean's small apartment was barely adequate for the two of them. When Helen moved in, she hadn't paid attention to the peeling wallpaper or the rusted water pipes. She overlooked the crowded bedroom and didn't mind that there was no room in the closet for her clothes. But lately, she was discovering that she disliked living out of a suitcase. It was time to find a place of her own.

Helen hadn't seen her mother since the day she visited and discovered that Clinton still lived in the house. She telephoned her father every week, and sometimes she would meet him on his streetcar and they'd talk while he drove the route. Helen asked him to leave Sarah and move into an apartment with her, but he wouldn't do it. He told Helen that she had a life to live, and she shouldn't be burdened by the likes of him. Helen hurt to see him so sad. She never asked about Sarah's boarder, and he never offered to discuss it.

During their times together, they talked about the cashier job and whether or not she was content. She assured him that she was getting along well, but it was still difficult whenever she thought of Bill. Michael's heart broke for her, and he wondered if any of them would ever find happiness.

1938

Mike Shea took care to press his shirt collar and wear the brown tie with the red dots. That was his favorite tie; he had gotten compliments from the girls in the office about how nice it looked. Before leaving for work, he put extra polish on his shoes and buffed them until they shone. Catching a glimpse of himself in the cracked mirror, he smoothed back his hair and patted a bit of cologne on his face. He decided that today he would ask her out on a date.

The coffee shop was unusually busy. Helen was tired from standing, and it was only noon; she had another four hours before closing time. Shifting her weight from one foot to the other, she saw him walk through the door and take a seat at the counter. He looked unusually frail today, and she noticed he needed a haircut. His shoes, although polished, were run down at the heels, and she could see he was due for a new pair. His suit jacket had been patched, the elbows were almost worn through. Funny, she had never noticed those things when he stood at the cash register to pay his bill.

Mike waited for the lunch crowd to thin. He saw how Helen smiled at all the customers. She seemed to brighten everyone's day. His palms were sweaty; he took the wrinkled handkerchief from his pocket to mop his brow. Thinking "now or never," he pushed himself up from the stool.

When Helen took the dollar from Mike, their hands touched for a moment, and Mike felt a shock wave all the way down to his feet. For the first time, he looked fully into her face and smiled. Surprised, she smiled back and

remarked that it was a lovely day, except for the smell outside. Her casual reference to the pungent stockyard odor
made him laugh. Taking a deep breath and letting it out
slowly, Mike asked Helen if she would have dinner with
him that evening. She hesitated a moment and then said,
"Yes."

Helen fussed with her hair and painted her nails. She
wore her best stockings, the ones with the dark seams;
although, you couldn't see much of them because her skirt
was just about five inches above her ankles. Helen prided
herself on dressing fashionably and liked for all heads to
turn when she walked down the street. She was a beautiful
woman.

Mike paced the sidewalk in front of her apartment. He
was early, and he didn't want to seem too anxious. He had
never been on a date with a woman before and hoped he
was doing the right thing. Mike saw something special in
Helen. He felt he could trust her. Nervous about seeing
her, yet feeling foolish for lingering, he climbed the stairs
and knocked on the door. He was ready to apologize for
being early, but he was surprised and delighted to see that
she was ready.

They relaxed over dinner and talked well into the
evening. They were comfortable sharing family stories.
Helen was careful to leave out the terrible parts about her
life with Sarah, but did tell him about Bill. It felt good to
talk to someone who seemed to understand. She hadn't
been able to open up to anyone since Bill's death, and it
was a relief to get it out. When Helen cried, Mike was
ready with a handkerchief. He told Helen about Kathleen,
how he had fallen in love, too. Listening to Mike, Helen

felt sorry for him, for she could hear the loneliness in his voice.

During their conversation, Helen couldn't help but notice how little he ate. His clean-shaven face was pale and gaunt under the glare of the restaurant lights, and she wondered if anyone at all looked in on him and if anyone cared about him.

The next time she saw her father, she told him about Mike. He was happy for Helen and glad to know that Mike was a full-blooded Irishman. They kept it from Sarah. She would only turn it into something ugly, and Helen didn't want Mike to know how awful her family was. She knew that other families had problems, but she couldn't imagine anyone's family being as crazy as hers. Once, when she and Mike stopped at her parents' house to drop off some prime cuts of meat, Helen introduced him as a friend. That bit of information satisfied her mother; she never asked Helen about him.

Now when Mike walked into the coffee shop, the real reason for coming was to talk to Helen. They began to see a lot of each other. Helen made soup in her apartment and took it to him; she cooked prime cuts of beef simmered in rich gravy. She boiled potatoes and vegetables and made sure his small icebox always had a pot of food for the hotplate. He appreciated her kindness, and he gave serious thought to asking her to marry him. It was risky, because he didn't know what he would do if she said no.

Helen was pleased that Mike was looking well. His face filled out a little, and his clothes fit him better. She found herself becoming fond of him. He was a gentleman. They shared wonderful evenings together, and she sensed that he was falling in love with her. She talked it over with her father. He liked Mike and thought she could do no better than to be married to a good man with a decent job. He also told her it was time to put Bill's memory aside and get on with her life.

Mike was paid well in his position as plant manager for Agar Meat Packing Company and had saved a good deal of money. It cost him very little to live, so he managed to put a large sum into the bank each week. He had visited Helen's parents' home a few times and saw that she had been raised in a nice house, and he knew he could give Helen all the lovely things she was used to. Mike was confident that he and Helen would have a good life together.

On his way home from work, he stopped at the jewelry store and picked out a beautiful platinum engagement ring. In the center sat a one-carat diamond. It was the most exquisite ring he had ever seen, and he hoped she would like it.

Parents
Married: September 2, 1938

MIKE CARBERRY SHEA

Born: September 20, 1900
            3715 U Street
            Omaha, Nebraska

Died: July 11, 1975

HELEN JEANETTE HEALY

Born: September 16, 1912
            915 Rush Street
            Chicago, Illinois

Died: September 17, 1988

Helen and Mike Shea celebrating New Year's Eve   1950s

An afternoon at Riverview Park in Chicago, Illinois in the year 1950. Helen and Mike with their four children—(from left) John Thomas, James Patrick, Bonnie Jean and Sharon Ann

EPILOGUE

The Ring
Portmagee,
County Kerry, Ireland

October 2004

As we drove up the road, we caught sight of the
Murphy cottage, familiar to us because we had
located it just five months before with the help of
Hannah's letter.

Now, standing on their doorstep, John and Kitty greeted
us with open arms. They welcomed our return and escorted
us into their parlor. The fire blazed, the crackling peat
spreading warmth across the room, drawing us in.
Comfortable overstuffed chairs looked recently fluffed, their
seat cushions beckoning us to sink in. Phil chose the chair
closest to the fire, and I sat on the couch across from him.

My cousin John joined me as I emptied my briefcase of
family papers. He reached for his glasses, happy to help
solve any of the remaining mysteries. Kitty disappeared
into the kitchen to prepare tea. She knew her tea and cakes
would be as welcome as the fire in the hearth.

I rolled out the land deeds from 1876 and showed John
the names of our Murphy families who had lived on

Ballyhearney. From there, we traced the years 1888, 1896 and so on, all the way to 1976. John was very interested and appreciative of the information revealed in the old deeds. He smiled when he heard names of the people he knew.

Kitty returned and announced that tea awaited us in the dining room. The aroma of good cooking laced with the sweet scent of the burning peat summoned us to the large wooden table set with beautiful china, patterned with Irish wildflowers.

We found the same seats we had sat in five months before, reminding me of family patterns. We chatted easily while reaching for the delicious slices of homemade fruit brack. Plump cherries, golden currants, and tiny brown raisins dotted the pound cake that was rapidly disappearing. Kitty remembered how much I enjoyed her cakes.

While I was stirring my tea and enjoying the conversation, Kitty got up from her chair and came to stand next to me. Bending over ever so slightly, she unfolded a soft white paper napkin and held it out on her open palm. She brought her hand closer to me. Like a spring flower, the napkin continued unfolding, and there in the center was revealed a gold wedding band. Kitty gestured that I should take it. She explained that this ring had belonged to my grandmother's sister Kate who had given it to Hannah, and Kitty felt that now it should be mine. In that instant, time slowed while Kitty placed this precious ring in my palm.

I heard muted conversation, but I saw only Kitty. We were the only two people in the room for those few seconds that it took me to realize what had just happened. When I looked into her eyes, there was love and acceptance, and I knew my journey to find my heritage had come full circle in this lovely cottage across from Ballyhearney.

Kitty returned to her chair. I wanted to replay the scene over and over again but knew it was impossible to recapture the experience of that moment. I held tight to the golden band that had been Aunt Kate's. My eyes locked with Kitty's and all the words that couldn't be said were felt by us at that moment.

This perfect symbol of love representing profound expressions of wholeness, unity, and completion affirmed my place with family. What began as a search evolved into a deep understanding of my grandparents' sacrifices, the hardships that made them the strong people they were, and the remarkable circumstances that brought me here to find my Irish.

Phil Bossard, my wonderful husband. He made this journey possible

At journey's end

Sources

National Archives, Bishop Street, Dublin
Website: www.nationalarchives.ie

General Register Office, Joyce House, Lombard St. East,
Dublin
Website: www.groireland.ie

National Library of Ireland, Kildare Street, Dublin
Website: www.nli.ie

Valuation Office, Irish Life Centre, Lower Abbey St.,
Dublin
Website: www.valoff.ie

Registry of Deeds, Henrietta Street, Dublin
Website: www.irlgov.ie/landreg/

County Libraries in Ireland and their University Libraries

The Emigrant Museum, Cobh, County Cork, Ireland

Ellis Island, New York
Website: ellisisland.org

Family History Center, 15 S. Temple St., Salt Lake City, Utah 84150
Website: www.familysearch.org

National Archives and Records Administration, Washington, D.C.
Website: www.nara.com

Chicago Historical Society Archives, Chicago, Illinois

Strokestown Famine Museum, County Roscommon, Ireland

Miller, Kerby, *Emigrants and Exiles*, Oxford University Press, 1985

MacAnnaidh, Seamas, *Irish History*, Paragon, 1999

Poirteir, Cathal, *Famine Echoes*, Gill & MacMillan, 1995

Woodham-Smith, Cecil, *The Great Hunger 1845-1849*, Penguin Books, 1962

Moylurg Writers, *Boyle*, 1988

Diner, Hasia, *Erin's Daughters in America*, Johns Hopkins University, 1983